O9-ABE-789

NNERS

Delicious Dinners for a Family
of Four that Don't Break the Bank

JULIE GRIMES

©2018 Time Inc. Books, a division of Meredith Corporation

Published by Oxmoor House, an imprint of Time Inc. Books,
a division of Meredith Corporation
225 Liberty Street, New York, NY 10281

All rights reserved. No part of this book may be reproduced in any form or by any
means without the prior written permission of the publisher, excepting brief quotations
in connection with reviews written specifically for inclusion in magazines or newspapers,
or limited excerpts strictly for personal use.

Senior Editor: Rachel Quinlivan West

Project Editor: Melissa Brown

Design Director: Melissa Clark

Photo Director: Paden Reich

Designer: Matt Ryan

Compositor: Teresa Cole

Photographers: Antonis Achilleos,
Caitlin Bensel, Jennifer Causey,
Steven DeVries, Kelsey Hansen,
Alison Miksch, Victor Protasio

Prop Stylists: Missie Neville Crawford,
Audrey Davis, Thom Driver,
Heather Chadduck Hillegas,
Mindi Shapiro Levine, Lindsey Lower,
Amy Stone, Kathleen Varner

Food Stylists: Margaret Monroe Dickey,
Anna Hampton, Rishon Hanners,
Karen Schroeder-Rankin, Tina Stamos,
Chelsea Zimmer

Recipe Testers: Robin Bashinsky,
Sarah Epperson, Paige Grandjean,
Adam Hickman, Julia Levy, Pam Lolley,
Laura Poythress, Kathy Sadler,
Marianne Williams, Deb Wise

Assistant Production Manager:
Diane Rose Keener

Associate Manager for Project Management
and Production: Anna Riego Muñiz

Copy Editors: Jacqueline Giovanelli,
Jasmine Hodges,

Proofreader: Donna Baldone

Indexer: Carol Roberts

Fellows: Kaitlyn Pacheco, Holly Ravazzolo

ISBN-13: 978-0-8487-5626-0
Library of Congress Control Number:
2018946268

First Edition 2018

Printed in the United States of America

10 9 8 7 6 5 4 3 2 1

We welcome your comments and
suggestions about Time Inc. Books.
Time Inc. Books
Attention: Book Editors
P.O. Box 62310
Tampa, Florida 33662-2310

Time Inc. Books products may be
purchased for business or promotional use.
For information on bulk purchases, please
contact Christi Crowley in the Special Sales
Department at (845) 895-9858.

CONTENTS

R0453109302

Roasted Brussels Sprouts with Bacon & Pecans (page 245)

Introduction

I spent my first decade living in Seagraves, a tiny West Texas town. My dad and granddad were farmer-ranchers, and our house was on the very edge of town. Just out back was a cattle pen. That's where my big sister, Christy, kept her prized 4H calf. Beyond that, our family farm stretched into the distance until the dusty red clay field met the sky.

Though Dad and Popa grew cash crops (cotton in the summers, wheat in the winters), there was always a veggie garden. My sisters and I picked okra and green beans from the small plot, piled them into a laundry basket (to measure a bushel) and stuffed paper grocery bags (for half-a-bushel). Then we'd load our red wagons and head out to sell our harvest. My younger sister, Catharine, and I served as Christy's cheap labor and made pennies on the dollar from our efforts. At least that's how I remember it. Christy says, "Y'all didn't work or get paid." Catharine says, "Christy paid us fair."

Popa, a red-haired Texas-Irish man, had a wicked sense of humor. My grandmother, Nanny, was often the butt of his (mostly) good-natured jokes. "Agnes is so tight, she'll squeeze a dollar bill 'til the eagle shits in her palm," he'd often brag, always with a proud chuckle.

In my opinion, Nanny's virtues were too many to count. Her frugality figured somewhere below her patience, kindness, and unending love for family. I always wanted to be just like her. A tall order, no doubt. And although I know I fall short of her grace in many—if not most—regards, I credit her for teaching me to cook. And how to be a tightwad.

Now that you've met most of the family, I have to give my mom her due. God bless her, she somehow managed to raise three rowdy daughters on her own, supporting us on her teacher's salary. Meanwhile, she also went to night classes and earned a master's degree. Oh, and she's not a cook. Hates it, actually. So thanks, Mom, for letting me do the cooking when I got old enough.

SECRETS OF A SUPERMARKET TIGHTWAD

I learned my first lessons in economics and budgeting while working on our family farm harvesting and selling our home-grown veggies and later walking the rows of cotton with a hoe, chopping weeds in the blazing Texas sun. We got paid about a quarter per row. Nanny, Queen of all Tightwads, was usually there with us too. What follows are many of her pearls of wisdom. I've picked up a few more pointers in the years since my days on the farm, so they're added in the mix also.

Plant a Garden

Or a fruit tree. At the very least, start a container garden with your favorite fresh herbs or small seasonal veggies.

Although I've been a city girl for all my adult life, I've always had a passion for growing my own food. I planted a fig tree in my backyard about the time my son Matthew was born. Later, Matthew and I planted a peach tree together. Now, years later, we still marvel each year as we wait anxiously for the fruit to ripen, so we can make ice cream and grill some fruit or sit together on a summer day and enjoy a bowl of peaches and cream, just like I used to do at Nanny and Popa's house back in Texas.

Another year on Mother's Day, Matthew and I created a raised bed and planted a backyard garden with eggplant, zucchini, several varieties of heirloom tomatoes, corn, and more. Some things thrived, while others, namely the corn, struggled, but tending that garden and watching Mother Nature work her magic filled us with wonder and gave us a mission each morning. And our meals were abundant and fresh.

At my business, Black Sheep Kitchen, I've upcycled an old ice bin into a small seasonal garden, so we have signs of life in the store and a few fresh ingredients to clip in a pinch. You can plant your fresh herbs in mason jars or portable pots, so you can pull them indoors during the winter months and still enjoy their fresh flavors year-round. If you buy fresh herbs in 3/4-ounce bags at the grocery (at $2.29 or more a pop), the savings add up quickly when you cross those off your shopping list. Not to mention there's less waste.

Go to the Source

Small farms, roadside stands, and farmers' markets are the best places to buy local, seasonal, fresh produce.

I remember a small peach orchard a few miles west of Seagraves. There weren't any U-Pick signs like you see at such places these days, but it was the same type deal. Every summer we piled into the car and drove out there while the trees were heavy with juicy, ripe, tangy-sweet peaches. We picked as much fruit as we could haul every trip. Once home, it was cobbler- and pie- and homemade ice cream-making time—a race against the clock to make good use of the precious summer bounty.

That's how I learned the importance of the fragrant smell of a ripe peach. Later, I realized that peaches, picked underripe and allowed to ripen off the tree, can eventually look and feel just like the ones we used to bring home from the orchard, but there's no way to fake that telltale scent.

I have no idea what we paid for the fruit we picked ourselves. But I know for a fact it was cheaper than the rock-hard, tasteless peaches on sale at the local grocery. Those were probably from California, picked before they were ready, and shipped all the way to Texas. Transportation and storage, that's what you pay for at the grocery, not flavor and fresh goodness.

Another benefit of going to the source is that you can build a relationship with your favorite farmers and support those who embody the ideals you believe in. The payoff here goes beyond your budget. Your new farmer friends can show you how to spot the best watermelons, and teach you that crowder peas are starchy, while lady peas have a delicate, almost sweet flavor. It's the best way to identify the sweetest local variety of peaches or plums and learn the exact window when they'll be at their best.

Shop in Season

Fresh produce is more expensive when it's sold out of season. Buy berries or figs in December, and you'll pay at least $1 more per pound. And like those California peaches that were sold in Texas, the winter berries and figs will be flavorless imposters with little likeness to glorious local summer fruits. Here's a chart to help you remember the natural growing season for a variety of fruits and vegetables.

SEASONAL FOOD GUIDE

SPRING	Artichokes, Asparagus, Beets, Carrots, English Peas, Fava Beans, Lettuces (arugula, spinach, watercress, and many greens are cool-weather crops), Mushrooms (especially morels), New Potatoes, Radishes, Ramps, Rhubarb, Spring Onions, Strawberries
SUMMER	Beans (string beans and shell beans), Blackberries, Blueberries, Cherries, Corn, Cucumbers, Eggplant, Field Peas, Figs, Melons, Okra, Peaches, Peppers, Plums, Plumcots (Pluots), Raspberries, Summer Squash, Tomatoes, Zucchini
FALL	Acorn Squash, Apples, Brussels Sprouts, Butternut Squash, Cranberries, Grapes, Kale, Lettuces, Mushrooms, Pears, Pumpkin, Spaghetti Squash, Sweet Potatoes
WINTER	Cabbage, Cauliflower, Clementines, Grapefruit, Meyer Lemons, Oranges, Parsnips, Persimmons, Pomegranates, Spaghetti Squash, Turnips, Winter Squash

Buy Whole Foods

This applies to everything from meats to veggies—anytime you buy pieces and parts (like boneless, skinless chicken breast or romaine hearts, for example), you'll pay more. It's less expensive to buy whole foods, like a whole chicken. Not to mention that meat roasted on the bone is always going to be tastier and more succulent than boneless cuts. Plus, you get the extras: After picking the carcass clean, use it to make stock, an essential ingredient for thrifty cooks.

Membership Has Its Privileges

It makes good sense and savings to buy frequently used staples in bulk, so shop for these ingredients at membership-based warehouses. Sam's Club, Costco, and BJ's Wholesale have membership fees, but regular shopping can net cash-back rewards.

I buy eggs at Sam's because two dozen organic eggs cost six bucks and change—less than the price of one dozen organic eggs at my local supermarket. Costco offers the best variety of lettuces. You'll find good prices on meats at both. If you're shopping for a special occasion, Costco carries prime-grade beef at great prices. It's rare to see prime beef anywhere other than on the menu at fancy restaurants. The best grade of beef most supermarkets and some butcher shops offer is choice, a step down from prime.

If storage space is the reason you don't buy in bulk, there are newish membership-based clubs cropping up on the web. Thrive Market, for example. At $59.95 per year, the membership cost is not drastically different from the brick-and-mortar clubs. There are many advantages to shopping at Thrive Market, including their focus on healthy foods, the fact that you won't have to buy in bulk, and you can purchase name-brand ingredients at least 25% cheaper than supermarket prices. For example, you can order Bob's Red Mill whole grains or King Arthur flours and baking mixes. And lots more.

Don't Skip Specialty Markets

Bulk sections and store brands at markets like Whole Foods often offer the best value on a variety of products, especially health foods. Shop bulk bins for whole grains and spices you don't use regularly. Though the price per ounce might cost more than that of prepackaged spices, you'll spend less if you buy only what you need for ingredients you may never use again. The 365 Whole Foods store brand offers affordable dairy products, like milk. Also, since Amazon bought Whole Foods, the prices of many items throughout the store have fallen.

Trader Joe's is an example of a national food market that's cracked the code on offering quality store-brand products intermixed with international imports, all at reasonable prices. For example, TJ's extra-virgin Spanish olive oil is my everyday olive oil. The flavor is good enough to work in cooking and cold/finishing applications alike. And the price! At $7.99 per 33.8-ounce bottle, it's hard to beat.

Be Seafood Savvy

Cost-cutting cooks tend to think they need to do without seafood. Not true. The seafood counter is the toughest part of the market to parse, but savvy shopping will save you a boatload.

While fresh halibut and wild salmon can be costly, there are plenty of other fish and shellfish in the seafood section. Freshwater options like trout and tilapia are cheaper than beef and available at markets nationwide. Sustainably farmed salmon delivers rich flavor at less than half the cost of wild-caught fillets. And even more savings await among the frozen options. Fresh food fanatics may balk, until they realize that the pristine fish they love at their favorite sushi place has all been flash-frozen as a food-safety measure. Flash freezing minimally affects the flavor and texture of fish, while dropping the supermarket price considerably.

Sustainable fishing practices are something else to consider. They do come with a price, so fresh-frozen is often the route for the budget-minded cook. There are a couple of exceptions. Fresh mollusks, like mussels or clams, are affordable and an environmentally friendly choice. And thanks to advances in inland fish-farming practices, both the variety and quality of farmed fresh fish are improving. Finding eco-friendly fish that are also economical is no easy task. Here are a few examples that fit the bill and are available in my area.

TYPE OF FISH	VARIETIES	OTHER INFO
Mollusks	Clams, mussels, oysters	
Freshwater fish	Trout, catfish, tilapia	
Meaty (ocean) fish	Atlantic mackerel*, Ahi Tuna (frozen)**, Sustainably farmed salmon	*low mercury risk **12 oz. = $4.99 @ Aldi
White flaky (ocean) fish	Alaskan cod (frozen)***	***$3.99/ lb. @ Trader Joe's
Shellfish	U.S. farmed shrimp	

If you can't find these same fish—or these same deals—in your area, here are good guidelines to follow:

1. The Marine Stewardship Council (https://www.msc.org) recognizes fisheries that use responsible practices. Look for MSC's logo and "Choose the Blue Fish" when you shop.

2. Aquaculture is the name of farmed fishing. Know you're buying from eco-friendly farmers when you see the Best Aquaculture Practices Certification (https://www.bapcertification.org).

3. When all else fails, check out the Monterey Bay Aquarium Seafood Watch (http://www.seafoodwatch.org).

YUMMY

Try New Things

If you usually stick to tenderloin and taters, premium fish, or other popular American fare, consider branching out. Experiment with less-expensive cuts of beef (see Butchers' Secrets, page 16). Try lesser-known varieties of fish, like fresh (or frozen or tinned) mackerel, for example. Or go meatless occasionally and expand your palate by sampling fruits, veggies, grains, and beans you've never tried. Your waistline and your wallet will thank you. The planet will too.

Being on a budget doesn't mean boring fare or being out of step with the latest food fads. In fact, you can stay on the culinary cutting edge by making DIY spice blends and pastes instead of buying pricey premixed varieties. For example, try my recipe for Homemade Harissa, a super flavorful, slightly spicy Mediterranean sauce, on page 116 and compare the cost to bottled versions sold on Amazon for about $12 for even a small jar.

> Try lesser-known varieties of fish, like fresh (or frozen or tinned) mackerel, for example.

Explore Ethnic Grocers

International markets serve up a world of flavor at a fraction of the cost vs. American supermarkets. Obviously, the local Asian and Latin markets in your city are the best, least-expensive places to find any ethnic ingredients, but many surprises lie in store as well. India is on the Asian continent, for instance, so you'll often find Indian ingredients at some Asian markets. Others are narrow and deep, like Great Wall Supermarket, a national chain that focuses mostly on Chinese foods. Likewise, H Mart, another national chain, specializes in Korean fare.

Shop Mediterranean markets for foods from any countries with borders that touch the sea. My local store offers a wide array of Middle Eastern ingredients and foods: from flatbreads and preserved lemons to a fully stocked meat counter.

Don't think exotic or esoteric ingredients are the only finds to be had at specialty markets though. I shop at Mi Pueblo—my favorite Latin market—on a regular basis. Of course, I always find beautiful fresh tomatillos, the best corn tortillas in town, and any fresh or dried chiles I need. Any Latin ingredient you can imagine is there. But there's more: fresh flat-leaf parsley for $0.89 per bunch, broccoli, eggplant, fresh fruits, and other common kitchen staples, like green onions, garlic, and more—up to 50% cheaper than grocery chains.

10 There's Always Room for Smart Splurges

Don't ever think that being on a budget means you can't afford the good stuff. You just have to plan and spend wisely. Take an inherently inexpensive dish, like pizza or pasta, and elevate it with a premium cheese, or a few slices of deliciously salty imported prosciutto. Here is a rundown of some premium ingredients that should be in every kitchen, no matter your budget.

Dijon mustard

The real French kind, such as Maille. Second best is Fallot, at World Market and Walmart.

Prosciutto

This prized ham produced in Parma, Italy, is the gold standard. If you can't find it, there are many country hams cured in the American South that make a delicious stand-in.

Parmigiano-Reggiano

The king of Italian cheeses, Parm-Reg is an aged cow's milk cheese with a trademark nutty flavor. Because it's been aged so long, the real stuff is crumbly when sliced and has a pleasantly gritty texture. It's also umami-rich, so this rock-star cheese adds a meaty flavor to any dish it graces, even vegetarian fare.

Gruyère

This is the best-quality, best-tasting Swiss cheese. Splurge on the real stuff where the cheese shines, but sub regular supermarket Swiss for casseroles and the like.

Cabot Seriously Sharp Cheddar

This white cheddar is produced in Vermont. Use it to make grilled cheese sandwiches, cheese spread, or to slice and enjoy with crackers for a snack. Otherwise, buy cheaper supermarket cheddar for most recipes. But always opt for sharp cheddar.

Toasted nut (and seed) oils

Although pricey, these oils offer unique and unrivaled flavor, and they're good for you to boot. Try pistachio oil tossed with rice or pasta. Drizzle toasted walnut oil over popcorn or use instead of olive oil to dress salads. There's no sub for dark sesame oil in Asian cooking (or any recipe, really).

Good-quality butter

I think European-style Plugra is the best, because its higher fat content produces a superior creamy flavor. My husband prefers butter made from grass-fed cattle, like Irish Kerrygold. His very favorite is tangy cultured butter made by a Southern artisan. Because these premium products have a higher price tag, use them only in recipes where you'll taste that difference. Generally, I reserve Plugra for baking, but I still don't use it in all baked goods.

Quality bacon

Although some brands are better than others, the most important consideration here is always use bacon that's smoked with real wood. Or choose bacon that is simply cured, not smoked at all. Artificial wood taste will overpower every dish. Every time.

Mayonnaise

Always use Hellmann's or Duke's. Period.

11 Move Over Pricey Protein

Most people would think there's no place for premium ingredients, like crabmeat, on a budget. Think again. There are several different types of crabmeat, and they come with a range of price tags. The most expensive: Colossal generally starts at about $30 per pound—understandably outside the tightwad's budget. But, crab's not off the menu altogether. If you're making a soup, for example, use backfin or claw meat, which is far less expensive.

Soups need only a small amount of crabmeat (or shrimp or other premium fish or shellfish), increasing your savings even more. Salads are like soups. You'll need only a bit of smoked salmon to toss into a salad to create a lovely—even healthy—budget-friendly meal that'll easily feed four.

Reconsider how you serve beef, pork, and chicken to realize even more savings. Instead of making these pricey proteins the center of the plate, shift to grain- and veggie-based dishes where meats play a supporting role. Try my Garlicky Spinach and Sausage Gratin (page 115) or Southwest Chicken & Quinoa Bowls (page 73) to get started.

BUTCHERS' SECRETS: THE UNUSUAL SUSPECTS

More cuts of beef are available to consumers now than ever before. Why? The cow hasn't changed, but the market has. As prices for premium cuts like tenderloin and even the once humble flank steak ballooned, demand for delicious meat has remained constant—or increased. And American butchers responded by letting us in on the fantastic meats they once saved for themselves.

These cuts come from the chuck and sirloin mostly. Treat these gems as you would a flank steak. All are thin lean cuts that taste best when cooked to no more than medium, preferably less. Medium-rare is best. And generally over fast, high heat—like the grill. Then let them rest briefly and slice them thinly against the grain for maximum tenderness.

Flap

Flap meat is also called flap steak, sirloin tip, and sirloin tip steak. Prices and sizes of this cut vary. It starts as low as $3.19 per pound. Get it while you can because, no doubt, as this cut gains popularity, prices will soar. When you find thicker flap roasts, take them home and cut your own steaks or ask your butcher to do it for you.

Flat Iron

This is cut from the shoulder with the grain. It's often confused with hanger steak because the long, thin rectangular shape is the same. Also called blade, top blade steak, oyster steak, or oyster blade.

Tri Tip

Californians have long used this lean triangular-shaped steak for their high-heat BBQ. And more recently it's started to make its way across the country. It's becoming known as a tasty and affordable cut for the grill. Also called Santa Maria steak and Newport Steak.

Merlot Steak

This supremely tender and flavorful steak comes from the cow's heel, just above the shank. The meat's fine grain is what makes it so tender, and like the other examples here, you don't want to overcook it for fear of damaging that lovely, velvety texture.

Petite Tender, Cap Steak, and the Denver Steak

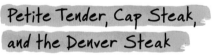

These cuts are flavorful up-and-comers on the steak scene, so if you see them, give them a try.

Stock Smartly

Making delicious, healthy, affordable meals for your family doesn't require expensive ingredients or specialty equipment. You'd be surprised at the variety of foods you can make with a minimally stocked kitchen. Here's my list of essentials to keep on hand at all times.

IN THE PANTRY

Seasonings, Spices & Dry Herbs

- Bay leaves
- Black peppercorns
- Crushed red pepper
- Dried oregano
- Garlic powder
- Ground cayenne pepper
- Ground cinnamon
- Ground cumin
- Ground ginger
- Kosher salt
- Smoked paprika
- Sweet paprika

Pasta, Rice & Other Grains

- Long pasta, like spaghetti or linguine
- Short pasta, like penne
- Long-grain white rice
- Brown rice
- Stone-ground grits or polenta
- Quinoa, farro, or your favorite whole grain
- Couscous

Vinegars & Oils

- Balsamic vinegar
- Cider vinegar
- Red wine vinegar
- White wine vinegar
- Distilled white vinegar
- Canola oil
- Extra-virgin olive oil

Other Goods

- Canned beans: black beans, cannellini, and chickpeas
- Canned whole peeled tomatoes
- Tomato paste
- Cornstarch
- Dijon mustard
- Honey
- Hot sauce
- Mayonnaise
- Panko breadcrumbs
- Soy sauce
- Cornmeal
- Olives: Kalamata and Castelvetrano
- Dried fruit: raisins, dried cherries
- Fresh onions: yellow, red
- Fresh garlic cloves
- Baking essentials: all-purpose flour; granulated, brown, and powdered sugar; baking powder and soda; pure vanilla extract, etc.

IN THE FRIDGE

- Large eggs
- Butter
- Bacon
- Lemons
- Carrots
- Celery
- Green onions
- Milk
- Cheese: sharp cheddar, Swiss, and Parmesan

IN THE FREEZER

- Shelled edamame
- Artichoke hearts
- English peas
- Nuts: almonds, pecans, walnuts (These aren't frozen when you buy them, but you can store them in the freezer to prevent them from going rancid.)

SPECIALTY INGREDIENTS FOR THE GOURMET

- Whole nutmeg
- Rice vinegar (unseasoned)
- Dark sesame oil
- Hoisin sauce
- Toasted walnut oil
- Dried porcini mushrooms or porcini powder
- Anchovy paste

Be a Bargain Hunter

Aldi is any tightwad's best friend. Hands down, their meat prices (and selection) are the best you'll find. The quality is good too. Definitely shop for nuts, common bottled spices, dried fruit, quinoa, and olives here. Aldi also has a small selection of good breads. Although seafood variety is limited, you should buy their frozen salmon and shrimp and fresh tilapia. Never buy goat cheese or Brie anywhere else. Produce is lacking and often picked over, but keep a keen eye out for sales and snap up the savings early in the day—shelves are restocked each morning. I avoid Aldi on weekends, though, as it's always packed.

Aldi is definitely worth a trip if you're within driving distance. If not, check out Walmart, where you'll find good quality and variety in the produce and meat departments.

And, of course, low prices throughout the store.

Also be aware of local grocery chains in your area that have bargain stores. It's worth searching them out and learning which items are cheaper, so you'll be in and out quickly when you make the trek.

> *Aldi is any tightwad's best friend. Hands down, their meat prices (and selection) are the best you'll find.*

How Total Costs are Calculated

I bought all ingredients to test and prepare these recipes at supermarkets, ethnic grocers, membership clubs, and bargain food marts like Aldi and Trader Joe's, all in the greater Birmingham, Alabama, area. A few other things you should know:

- No items were purchased on sale, so when you find sales, you'll save even more.
- The cost per meal reflects only the prices for specific amounts of each ingredient needed to prepare the recipes.
- Also, about those total costs, any sides listed as options to serve with the entrées are included in the total cost of the meal. Any variations or alternatives given for those sides are not. Every side costs around $4 or less to prepare.
- Each recipe feeds at least four—some yield more.

HOW LOW CAN YOU GO?

Within each chapter, you'll find a recipe or two with the "How Low Can You Go" tag to call attention to the least-expensive recipes in each bunch.

Cauliflower Rice,
page 203

Pizza and pasta are perennial favorites at the American dinner table. The starchy base for each—noodles or crust—is like a blank canvas you can adorn with flavors and toppings you love to create the ultimate family-friendly masterpiece. Both can go haute or homey, depending on your audience. Pick your favorite style of crust—bubbly, charred, and deliciously chewy Neapolitan; sturdy and thin-ish New York–style; or paper-thin and shatteringly crisp Cracker Crust—and bake a perfect pie in the comfort of your kitchen for a sliver of the price of delivery or dining out. No need to head to a white-tablecloth Italian eatery when you can prepare prize-worthy pasta at home.

Total Cost $0.75

New York–Style Pizza Dough

HANDS-ON 20 MIN.
TOTAL 1 HR., 25 MIN.
MAKES DOUGH FOR
1 (12- TO 14-INCH) PIE

Weigh or lightly spoon 1 cup all-purpose flour (about 4.5 ounces) into a dry measuring cup; level with a knife. Combine 1 cup flour, 1 teaspoon sugar, 1 package active dry yeast (about 2 1/4 teaspoons), and 1 cup warm water (100° to 110°F) in a mixing bowl; let stand 15 minutes. Weigh or lightly spoon 2 2/3 cups flour (about 12 ounces) into dry measuring cups; level with a knife. Combine 2 2/3 cups flour and 1 1/2 teaspoons kosher salt in a large bowl; make a well in the center of the mixture. Add the yeast mixture, 1/2 cup warm water, and 2 tablespoons olive oil to the flour mixture; stir well. Turn the dough out onto a floured surface. Knead until smooth and elastic (about 10 minutes); add enough flour, 1 tablespoon at a time (up to 1/3 cup), to prevent the dough from sticking to your hands (dough will feel tacky). Place the dough in a large bowl coated with cooking spray, turning to coat top. Cover and let rise in a warm place (85°F), free from drafts, 45 minutes or until doubled in size. (Press two fingers into the dough. If the indentation remains, then the dough has risen enough.) Punch the dough down. Roll the dough out to a 12- to 14-inch circle on a flat surface covered with 2 tablespoons cornmeal; cover and let stand 20 minutes. Proceed with the desired pizza recipe.

Total Cost: $0.84

Neapolitan-Style Pizzeria Dough

HANDS-ON 15 MIN.
TOTAL 1 HR., 40 MIN. PLUS 24 HR.
MAKES DOUGH FOR
1 (12- TO 14-INCH) PIE

Pour 1/2 cup warm water (100° to 110°F) in the bowl of a stand mixer with the dough hook attached. Weigh or lightly spoon 2 1/4 cups bread flour (about 10.68 ounces) into dry measuring cups; level with a knife. Add the flour to the mixing bowl, but do not stir. Cover and let stand 20 minutes. Combine 1/4 cup warm water and 1 package active dry yeast (about 2 1/4 teaspoons) in a small bowl; let stand 5 minutes or until bubbly. Scrape the yeast mixture into mixing bowl. Add 2 teaspoons kosher salt to the flour mixture; mix 5 minutes on medium or until a soft dough forms. Place the dough in a large bowl coated with 1 tablespoon extra-virgin olive oil; cover the surface of the dough with plastic wrap that's coated with cooking spray. Refrigerate for 24 to 48 hours. Remove the dough from the refrigerator. Let stand, covered, 1 hour or until the dough comes to room temperature. Punch the dough down. Sprinkle 1 tablespoon cornmeal over a lightly floured baking sheet without raised sides. Press the dough out to a 12- to 14-inch circle on prepared pan. Crimp edges to form a 1/2-inch border. Cover dough loosely with plastic wrap while oven preheats. Proceed with the desired pizza recipe.

Total Cost: $0.39

Cracker Crust Pizza Dough

HANDS-ON 20 MIN.
TOTAL 1 HR., 25 MIN. PLUS 24 HR.
MAKES DOUGH FOR
1 (12- TO 14-INCH) PIE

Combine 1/2 cup warm water (100° to 110°F) and 1/2 teaspoon active dry yeast in the bowl of a stand mixer with the dough hook attached; let stand 5 minutes or until bubbly. Add 2 tablespoons extra-virgin olive oil and 1/4 teaspoon kosher salt to the yeast mixture. Weigh or lightly spoon 1 1/4 cups all-purpose flour (about 5.63 ounces) into dry measuring cups; level with a knife. Sprinkle the flour over the yeast mixture; mix 2 minutes or until a soft dough forms. Place the dough in a large bowl coated with cooking spray; cover the surface of the dough with plastic wrap lightly coated with cooking spray. Refrigerate for 24 hours. Remove the dough from the refrigerator. Let stand, covered, 1 hour or until the dough comes to room temperature. Sprinkle 1 tablespoon cornmeal over a lightly floured flat surface. Punch the dough down; roll out to a very thin (1/8- to 1/16-inch thickness) 14-inch circle on the prepared surface. Crimp the edges to form a 1/2-inch border. Pierce the dough several times with a fork. Transfer the dough to a preheated pizza stone or baking sheet, and proceed with the desired pizza recipe.

New York-Style Pizza Dough

The thin, sturdy crust allows each piece to stand at attention when you pick it up. Although the crust crackles slightly when you make the requisite (lengthwise) fold and bite into it, it's by no means so crisp that the slice cracks or breaks down the seam.

Cracker Crust Pizza Dough

I turn to this crust for minimally or entirely unsauced pies. I also tend to pair it with nontraditional toppers, although you can use this crust in any way you see fit.

Neapolitan-Style Pizzeria Dough

If you love blistered, puffy, chewy pizza, use this dough. Ideal for the planners of the world, this dough is easy to make, but needs to rest for at least 24 hours before you roll and bake your pie.

Summer Veggie Pizza

Total cost $8.69

HANDS-ON **25 MIN.**   TOTAL **40 MIN.**   SERVES **4**

New York–style crust is best for this pizza because it'll hold the weight of all the colorful fresh veggies on top. This is a good choice for a fun pizza night or party: Divide the dough into balls for individual pizzas, and let everyone choose his or her own toppings. Serve this with Spinach & Herb Salad with Strawberry Vinaigrette (page 194). You'll also want to plan ahead and make a batch of Strawberry Lemonade Jam (page 217), so it'll be chilled and ready for you to prepare a zingy dressing for the salad. For a fall and winter pizza variation, omit the asparagus, corn, and mozzarella, and add 2 cups cooked cubed butternut squash and ³/₄ cup shredded Swiss cheese to the pizza before baking.

3 tablespoons olive oil, divided

2 garlic cloves, peeled and crushed

1 cup sliced onion

1 red bell pepper, cut into thin strips

8 ounces asparagus, trimmed and cut into 1-inch pieces

2 ears corn

1 tablespoon cornmeal

New York–Style Pizza Dough (page 22)

4 ounces fresh mozzarella cheese, sliced

1 teaspoon kosher salt

¹/₂ teaspoon crushed red pepper

2 tablespoons small fresh basil leaves

1. Preheat the oven to 500°F.

2. Heat a small skillet over medium heat. Add 2 tablespoons olive oil and the garlic to the pan; cook 2 minutes or until fragrant (do not brown). Remove the garlic from the oil, and reserve the garlic for another use. Remove the garlic oil from pan; set aside.

3. Increase the heat to medium-high. Add the remaining 1 tablespoon oil to the pan; swirl to coat. Add the onion and bell pepper; sauté 5 minutes. Place the onion mixture in a bowl. Add the asparagus to the bowl. Cut the corn from the cobs; add the corn to the bowl with the veggies.

4. Scatter the cornmeal over a lightly floured surface; roll the dough into a 13-inch circle on the prepared surface. Transfer the dough to a baking sheet; brush the dough with the garlic oil. Top with the vegetable mixture, leaving a ¹/₂-inch border; sprinkle the cheese, salt, and pepper over the top. Bake at 500°F for 15 minutes or until golden. Top with the basil. Cut into 8 slices.

TIGHTWAD TIP
Don't Buy What You Can DIY

- Make your own crust. It costs less than a buck to make (see page 22). If you can find a store-bought dough that tastes as good for less, snap it up, but that's not likely.

- Make your own sauce. All-Purpose Tomato Sauce (page 221) is a great place to start. But think beyond traditional red sauce by using Alabama-Style White BBQ Sauce (page 222) or your favorite BBQ sauce or salad dressing.

- Make your own soft cheese to spread over your pie. See Lemon Ricotta (page 210).

Two-Cheese Lemony Broccolini Pizza

Total cost $8.00

HANDS-ON **30 MIN.**   TOTAL **1 HR., 50 MIN.**   SERVES **4**

Look for Broccolini in the produce section. If you can't find it, sub broccoli florets or try pleasantly bitter broccoli rabe. Serve with Orzo-Tomato Toss.

Neapolitan-Style Pizzeria Dough
  (page 22)

1 bunch Broccolini, trimmed and cut
  into 1-inch pieces

3 tablespoons canola oil

2 large garlic cloves, smashed

2 tablespoons cornmeal

1/2 cup Lemon Ricotta
  (page 210)

1/2 cup vertically sliced red onion

1/2 cup coarsely chopped walnuts

3 ounces fresh mozzarella, thinly
  sliced

1 green onion, sliced

TIGHTWAD TIP
Fresh Mozzarella

A ball of creamy, snow-white fresh mozzarella is leagues above the yellowish blocks of mozzarella in both flavor and texture. Problem is: Fresh mozz is also generally quite a bit more expensive. Not anymore! Aldi sells 8-ounce packages of fresh mozzarella for $1.99 ($0.25 per ounce). Walmart doesn't beat (or match) that price.

1. Remove the dough from the refrigerator, and let stand at room temperature for 1 hour or until completely thawed to room temperature.

2. Place a pizza stone or pizza pan in the oven; preheat the oven and pan to 500°F.

3. Meanwhile, blanch the Broccolini for 1 minute in boiling salted water; drain. Rinse the Broccolini with cold running water; pat dry. Combine the canola oil and garlic in a small pan over medium heat; bring to a simmer. Remove from the heat; let stand 5 minutes. Discard the garlic.

4. Place a sheet of parchment paper on a flat surface; sprinkle the cornmeal over the parchment. Roll the dough out to a 12- to 14-inch circle on the prepared parchment. Brush the garlic oil over the prepared crust; dot the ricotta around the pizza. Arrange the Broccolini, sliced onion, and nuts on the pizza in a single layer; top with the mozzarella. Using the parchment paper, slide the pizza onto the preheated stone or pan; bake at 500°F for 12 to 15 minutes or until the crust is blistered and cooked through. Sprinkle with the green onions, slice, and serve.

SERVE WITH
Orzo-Tomato Toss

Toss together 1 cup hot cooked orzo pasta and Marinated Tomatoes (page 209). Serves 4

Smoked Salmon Cracker Crust Pizza

Total cost **$9.96**

HANDS-ON **16 MIN.**   TOTAL **25 MIN.**   SERVES **4**

The pizza is delicious, but a little light—you'll need a hearty side to fill up the fam. Fattoush, Mediterranean pita bread tossed with herbs, veggies, and tasty, tangy dressing is what inspired the yummy salad. Feel free to improvise on the theme. Swap tomatoes for cucumber, for example, or use another herb. Whatever suits your mood and your family's taste buds. Serve with the Mediterranean Pita Salad.

Cracker Crust Pizza Dough (page 22)

$1/2$ cup (4 ounces) cream cheese, softened

2 tablespoons capers, drained

4 ($1/8$-inch-thick) slices red onion, separated into rings

3.5 ounces thinly sliced smoked salmon

1 tablespoon chopped fresh dill

TIGHTWAD TIP
Make One Flavor Shine

Decide what one flavor you want to stand out in your dish, and then splurge on that and scrimp on the rest. For example, shave good imported Parmigiano-Reggiano over the top of pizza or salad for a finishing flourish you can see and taste.

1. Preheat the oven to 550°F. Place a pizza stone in the oven while it preheats.

2. Roll the dough out on a lightly floured surface to a $1/8$- to $1/16$-inch thickness. Slide the dough onto the preheated pizza stone, using a spatula as a guide. Bake at 550°F for 4 minutes. Remove from the oven; spread the cream cheese evenly over the dough. Arrange the capers and onion over the cheese. Bake 5 more minutes or until the crust is golden brown. Top with the salmon; sprinkle with the dill. Cut into 8 slices. Serve immediately.

SERVE WITH
Mediterranean Pita Salad

Preheat the oven to 425°F. Coarsely chop 2 (6-inch) pita breads; toss with 1 tablespoon extra-virgin olive oil, and sprinkle lightly with salt and pepper. Spread the pita in a single layer on a baking sheet; bake at 425°F for 5 to 7 minutes or until lightly toasted. Whisk together 1 tablespoon extra-virgin olive oil, 2 teaspoons fresh lemon juice, and 1 teaspoon minced fresh garlic. Add toasted pita, 1 chopped plum tomato, 1 thinly sliced green onion, $1/4$ cup halved pitted kalamata olives, and 2 tablespoons chopped fresh flat-leaf parsley leaves; toss. Drain and rinse 1 (15.5-ounce) can chickpeas; add to salad. Sprinkle $1/4$ cup crumbled feta over salad, and season to taste with salt and pepper. Serve immediately. Serves 4

White Chicken Pizza with Wilted Spinach

Total cost $6.05

HANDS-ON **17 MIN.** TOTAL **30 MIN.** SERVES **4**

This recipe is like pizza and a salad all in one, so you don't have to worry about making anything else to serve with it. Here is an instance where I use more expensive Gruyère cheese instead of generic Swiss for the flavor boost. Scout for the best prices on Gruyère at Walmart, Sam's, and Costco.

2 teaspoons canola oil

2 boneless, skinless chicken thighs, cut into bite-sized pieces

1/2 teaspoon kosher salt

1/2 teaspoon freshly ground black pepper

2 teaspoons minced fresh garlic

Neapolitan-Style Pizzeria Dough (page 22)

1 cup Alabama-Style White BBQ Sauce (page 222)

3/4 cup shredded Gruyère cheese

Wilted Spinach Salad

1. Preheat the oven to 500°F. Place a pizza stone or round pizza pan in the oven while it preheats.

2. Heat a small sauté pan over medium-high heat. Add the oil to the pan; swirl to coat. Sprinkle the chicken with 1/2 teaspoon each of salt and pepper, and brown in the hot oil for 2 to 3 minutes, turning to brown on all sides. Add the garlic; sauté 30 seconds, stirring constantly. Remove from the heat.

3. Roll the dough out on a lightly floured surface to a 14-inch circle. Slide the dough onto the preheated pizza stone, using a spatula as a guide. Spread the sauce evenly over the dough, leaving a 1-inch border. Arrange the chicken mixture over the dough, and sprinkle with the cheese. Bake at 500°F for 13 to 15 minutes or until the crust is blistered and cooked through.

4. Meanwhile, prepare the Wilted Spinach Salad. Scatter over the cooked pizza. Slice pizza into 8 slices. Serve immediately.

SERVE WITH
Wilted Spinach Salad

Cook 2 slices bacon in a sauté pan over medium heat until crisp, about 6 minutes. Remove bacon from pan; reserve the drippings in the pan. Drain bacon; crumble. Sauté 1 cup thinly sliced red onion in drippings over medium-high heat for 1 to 2 minutes, just until starting to soften. Add 1 1/2 tablespoons sugar and 3 tablespoons cider vinegar; bring to a boil, stirring constantly. Remove from the heat, and toss hot dressing with 3 cups baby spinach; season to taste with salt and pepper. Top with bacon. Serves 4

Sausage & Onion Pizza with Cauliflower Crust

Total cost $9.75

HANDS-ON 35 MIN.　TOTAL 1 HR., 15 MIN.　SERVES 4

If you don't want to make All-Purpose Tomato Sauce, buy a small jar of pizza or marinara sauce. But remember, convenience costs more. Serve with Garlicky Toast on page 202.

3 tablespoons canola oil, divided

4 cups coarsely shredded cauliflower

3/4 teaspoon kosher salt

1 tablespoon butter

2 teaspoons minced fresh garlic, divided

1/4 cup grated Parmesan cheese (about 1 ounce)

2 large eggs

Cooking spray

2 (4-ounce) links mild Italian pork sausage, casings removed

8 ounces sliced white mushrooms

3 cups sliced onion (about 2 medium)

1 teaspoon balsamic vinegar

2/3 cup All-Purpose Tomato Sauce (page 221) or store-bought

4 ounces fresh mozzarella cheese, thinly sliced

Shredding Cauliflower

A food processor shreds cauliflower easily. If you have attachments with different-sized holes, choose the larger one to produce a coarse texture. Too fine, and it'll produce a wet and mushy crust.

1. Preheat the broiler to high. Place a pizza stone on the bottom rack of the oven while it preheats.

2. Line a baking sheet with foil; brush with 1 tablespoon oil. Spread the cauliflower on the pan; sprinkle with the salt. Broil 8 to 10 minutes or until golden, rotating pan after 5 minutes.

3. Meanwhile, melt the butter in a small pan over medium heat. Add 1 teaspoon garlic to the pan; cook 30 seconds or just until fragrant, stirring constantly. Remove from the heat; let stand 5 minutes. Place the cauliflower mixture in a bowl; stir in the garlic butter. Cool 15 minutes.

4. Reduce the oven temperature to 450°F.

5. Add the Parmesan and eggs to the cauliflower; stir well. Press cauliflower mixture into a 12-inch circle on parchment paper coated with cooking spray. Slide the parchment onto the preheated stone. Return to oven; bake at 450°F for about 8 minutes or until lightly browned and set.

6. Meanwhile, heat a medium sauté pan over medium-high heat. Add 1 tablespoon oil; swirl to coat. Add the sausage; sauté 3 minutes or until browned, stirring to crumble. Add the mushrooms; sauté 4 minutes or until tender. Add the remaining 1 teaspoon garlic; sauté 2 minutes or until sausage is done. Remove mixture from pan; set aside. Wipe pan clean.

7. Set the pan over medium-high heat. Add the remaining 1 tablespoon oil; swirl to coat. Add the onion; sauté 6 minutes or until the onion is browned, stirring occasionally. Add the vinegar; sauté 2 minutes or until the onion is soft.

8. Spread the sauce over the crust, leaving a 1/2-inch border. Top with the onion and sausage mixture. Top with mozzarella. Bake at 450°F for 10 to 12 minutes or until browned. Cut into 8 slices.

Roasted Cauliflower Pasta

Total cost $9.70

HANDS-ON **20 MIN.**   TOTAL **40 MIN.**   SERVES **4**

If you've never roasted cauliflower before, you're in for a tasty surprise. At my house, we use this technique all the time, and I'm still surprised how something so simple can be so darn delicious. There are a couple of keys to success: Get your roasting pan good and hot before adding the cauliflower. Be sure to get your cut, flat surfaces on the cauliflower in contact with the surface of the hot pan. And don't pull the pan from the oven until you think you may have burned it smack up. Seriously. Deep color on the veggies equals deep flavor. When you shop for this recipe, you can get domestic Parmesan cheese for the breadcrumbs—it's cheaper. But splurge on a small chunk of the good, imported, aged Parm-Reg to shave over the top. Serve with Celery-Apple Salad on page 187.

4 cups cauliflower florets

1 small red onion, cut into wedges

5 tablespoons extra-virgin olive oil, divided

5 teaspoons kosher salt, divided

8 ounces uncooked penne pasta

²/₃ cup pitted kalamata olives, halved

¹/₃ cup golden raisins

2 teaspoons chopped fresh thyme

1 teaspoon grated fresh lemon zest

¹/₄ teaspoon crushed red pepper

¹/₂ cup Parsley & Parmesan Breadcrumbs (page 225)

2 ounces Parmigiano-Reggiano, shaved

1. Preheat the oven to 450°F. Place a shallow roasting pan in the oven while it preheats.

2. Toss the cauliflower and onion wedges with 2 tablespoons oil. Spread the cauliflower mixture in the preheated pan. Roast at 450°F for 20 to 25 minutes or until the veggies are tender and golden, stirring after 10 minutes.

3. Meanwhile, bring 8 cups water and 1¹/₂ tablespoons kosher salt to a boil in a medium saucepan. Add the pasta, and cook until almost al dente, about 7 to 8 minutes. Drain the pasta, reserving ¹/₂ cup pasta cooking water. Return the pasta water to the saucepan, and bring to a boil over medium-high heat. Stir in the remaining 3 tablespoons oil; boil until water reduces by half and a silky sauce forms. Return the pasta to the sauce; cook until the sauce coats the pasta. Remove from the heat.

4. Stir in the remaining ¹/₂ teaspoon salt, olives, and the next 4 ingredients. Season to taste with salt and black pepper. Spoon pasta into a serving dish; top with the breadcrumbs and cheese. Serve immediately.

Get Saucy

Pasta sauces are easy to make at home without breaking your budget. One way is to reserve some starchy pasta cooking water, and enrich it with olive oil, butter, or eggs to build a rich, silky sauce that costs just pennies. Using salty pasta cooking water as the sauce base creates robust flavor, allowing you to use fewer quantities of more expensive ingredients, like cheese.

Corkscrew Pasta with Pistachio Pesto

Total cost $10.00

HANDS-ON **30 MIN.**   TOTAL **30 MIN.**   SERVES **4**

Finish this lively pasta with a crumble of soft cheese over the top. I love goat cheese because it's tangy and pairs nicely with the lemon note in the pesto. Use feta or big rustic shavings of an aged cheese, like Parm, if you prefer. You'll want to keep this Pistachio Pesto in your regular rotation. It's dead simple, but amazingly bright, fresh, and flavorful. Dollop it on basic grilled or roasted meats, or toss it with grilled shrimp. Enliven steamed veggies or plain hot cooked rice by tossing with a couple of spoonfuls. Round out this pasta meal with Roasted Green Beans with Browned Butter on page 195—buy haricots verts (tiny French green beans) if you can find them.

1 ½ tablespoons kosher salt

8 ounces uncooked cavatappi (corkscrew) or penne pasta

2 tablespoons unsalted butter

Pistachio Pesto

3 cups halved cherry tomatoes

2 cups baby kale

1 (15-ounce) can cannellini beans, drained and rinsed

2 ounces crumbled goat cheese

1. Bring 8 cups water and 1 ½ tablespoons kosher salt to a boil in a medium saucepan. Add the pasta, and cook until almost al dente, about 7 to 8 minutes. Drain the pasta, reserving ½ cup pasta cooking water. Return the pasta water to the pan, and stir in the butter. Cook over medium-high heat, whisking until the butter melts; cook 30 seconds. Return the cooked pasta to the pan; cook about 1 minute or until the pasta absorbs most of the liquid, tossing constantly. Remove from the heat. Transfer the pasta mixture to a large mixing bowl.

2. Add the pesto, tomatoes, kale, and beans to the pasta; toss to coat. Season to taste with salt and pepper; toss. Sprinkle with the goat cheese.

Pistachio Pesto

Place ½ cup shelled, roasted salted pistachios, 1 tablespoon minced fresh shallot, 2 ½ teaspoons grated fresh lemon zest, and 2 teaspoons coarsely chopped fresh garlic in a mini chopper; process until finely ground, scraping sides as necessary. With motor running, gradually add 3 tablespoons extra-virgin olive oil, processing until a fine paste forms, scraping sides as needed. Makes about ½ cup

Spaghetti & Meatballs

HANDS-ON **25 MIN.**   TOTAL **40 MIN.**   SERVES **4**

Total cost
$8.37

Whip up Caesar Salad with Garlicky Croutons & Homemade Dressing (page 194) to serve with this classic pasta. Double the meatball mixture and freeze some for later. Serve them in soups or over roasted spaghetti squash. You can also make a meatball sub topped with sauce and cheese.

1 tablespoon canola oil

³/₄ cup finely chopped yellow onion (1 small onion)

¹/₃ cup finely diced, peeled carrot (about 1 large)

¹/₃ cup Overnight Chicken Stock (page 218) or store-bought

¹/₂ teaspoon freshly ground black pepper

2 ³/₄ cups All-Purpose Tomato Sauce (page 221) or store-bought, divided

3 tablespoons chopped fresh basil, divided

1 ¹/₂ teaspoons kosher salt, divided

¹/₄ cup grated Parmesan cheese, divided

1 tablespoon minced fresh garlic

1 large egg

12 ounces ground chuck

¹/₈ teaspoon crushed red pepper

12 ounces uncooked spaghetti

1. Preheat the oven to 400°F.

2. Heat the oil in a 4-quart saucepan over medium-high heat. Add the onion and carrot; cook, stirring frequently, until softened, 5 to 6 minutes. Transfer the onion mixture to a medium mixing bowl. Return the pan to medium heat, and add the stock, pepper, 2 ¹/₄ cups tomato sauce, 1 tablespoon basil, and 1 teaspoon salt. Bring to a simmer, reduce the heat to medium-low, and cook, stirring occasionally until slightly thickened, about 20 minutes.

3. Add the remaining ¹/₂ cup tomato sauce, 1 tablespoon basil, 3 tablespoons cheese, garlic, and egg to the bowl with onion mixture; stir well. Add the beef, red pepper, and the remaining ¹/₂ teaspoon salt; mix gently until just combined. Shape into 16 (about 1-ounce) meatballs, and place on a parchment paper–lined baking sheet. Bake at 400°F until the meatballs are cooked through, 12 to 14 minutes. Let the meatballs cool on the baking sheet for 5 minutes. Gently add the meatballs to the pan with the sauce.

4. Cook the pasta in boiling salted water according to the package directions; drain. Divide the pasta evenly among 4 plates; top each serving with 4 meatballs and sauce. Sprinkle the remaining 1 tablespoon cheese and 1 tablespoon basil evenly among the bowls. Serve immediately.

TIGHTWAD TIP
Ground Beef

Next time you're standing at the meat counter at your local supermarket, take a good look at the choices of ground beef. The 80/20 (80% lean) blend is your best option for a couple of reasons: It's less expensive than the leaner varieties, and ground beef needs a little fat to give it flavor. And although it's slightly more expensive than even fattier grinds, the 80/20 blend is just the right mix for moist, flavorful meatballs that aren't excessively greasy.

Winter Veggie Carbonara

Total cost
$7.22

HANDS-ON **35 MIN.**   TOTAL **40 MIN.**   SERVES **4**

Italian cooks have a tradition of *cucina povera*. The literal translation is "cooking of the poor." Thrifty Italian cooks have taken a nose-to-tail approach to cooking for centuries, leaving no scraps to waste. The classic version of carbonara uses guanciale, cured pig's jowl. My version takes that thrifty spirit one step further by adding veggies for a hearty one-dish meal that's company worthy.

3 slices applewood-smoked bacon

1 pound fresh Brussels sprouts, trimmed and halved

2 tablespoons kosher salt

8 ounces uncooked fettuccine

2 ounces grated Pecorino-Romano cheese

1 large egg

1 large egg yolk

3 cups trimmed, sliced fresh rainbow chard

1 teaspoon grated fresh lemon zest

1/8 teaspoon crushed red pepper

🛍️ TIGHTWAD TIP
💲 Pecorino-Romano

Try Pecorino-Romano, a less expensive alternative to Parmigiano-Reggiano cheese. Pecorino is an aged sheep's milk cheese with a salty flavor and slightly grainy texture that's similar to Parm-Reg. Like most sheep's milk cheeses, Pecorino is pungent, so a little goes a long way—terrific for a thrifty cook.

1. Preheat the oven to 425°F.

2. Arrange the bacon in a single layer in a small shallow roasting pan. Bake at 425°F for 12 minutes or until the bacon is crisp, turning after 6 minutes. Remove the bacon from the pan, reserving the drippings in the pan. Cool and crumble the bacon.

3. Add the Brussels sprouts to the drippings in the pan. Sprinkle with salt and black pepper to taste; toss. Roast the Brussels sprouts at 425°F for 10 to 12 minutes or until golden and crisp-tender, stirring after 6 minutes. Place in a bowl, and top with the crumbled bacon.

4. Bring 8 cups water and 2 tablespoons kosher salt to a boil in a 12-inch straight-sided sauté pan over medium-high heat. Add the pasta, and cook just until al dente, about 10 minutes, stirring occasionally to prevent the pasta from clumping. Drain the pasta, reserving 1/2 cup pasta cooking water.

5. Combine the cheese, egg, and yolk in a heat-safe medium bowl. Ladle the reserved pasta water, 2 ounces at a time, into the egg mixture, whisking constantly to gradually increase the temperature of eggs without scrambling them. Return the pasta to sauté pan over low heat. Add the egg mixture to pan and cook over low heat for 1 to 2 minutes, just until the sauce begins to thicken and coat the pasta, tossing constantly. Add the Brussels sprouts and chard; toss. Remove from the heat; stir in the zest, red pepper, and additional black pepper. Serve immediately.

Fettuccine with Squash Noodles & Kale Pesto

Total cost $9.79

HANDS-ON 25 MIN.   TOTAL 35 MIN.   SERVES 4

If you don't have a spiralizer, you can buy one at kitchen emporiums like Bed, Bath & Beyond or Williams-Sonoma. Or just use your vegetable peeler to make squash ribbons instead. You can also spoon the Kale Pesto over goat cheese, serve it with bread or crackers, stir it into softened butter, or dollop on top of hot grilled or roasted meats. Buy a carton of cherry or grape tomatoes while you're shopping for this recipe, and make crazy-good Blistered Tomatoes (page 202) to serve with a baguette and your pasta supper.

3 $^3/_4$ teaspoons kosher salt, divided

8 ounces uncooked fettuccine

1 medium zucchini

1 medium-sized yellow squash

2 tablespoons unsalted butter

Kale Pesto

$^1/_2$ teaspoon freshly ground black pepper

1. Bring 4 quarts water and 1 tablespoon salt to a boil in a medium saucepan. Add the pasta; cook until almost al dente, about 7 $^1/_2$ minutes. Drain the pasta, reserving 1 cup pasta cooking water.

2. Run the zucchini and squash through the medium shredder blade of a spiralizer to form long strands.

3. Return the reserved pasta water to pan over medium-high heat; bring to a boil. Add the butter, and boil 1 minute or until the butter is melted and emulsified into the water. Add the pasta; cook 30 seconds, tossing until a thin sauce clings to the noodles. Add the zucchini and squash; toss. Remove from the heat; toss with the pesto. Season with the remaining $^3/_4$ teaspoon salt and the pepper.

Kale Pesto

Trim 9 ounces fresh kale. Blanch the kale in boiling salted water for 1 minute; drain. Rinse with cold water; drain. Place the blanched kale, 1 $^1/_2$ teaspoons kosher salt, $^1/_3$ cup grated Parmesan cheese, $^1/_4$ cup chopped toasted walnuts, 1 tablespoon grated fresh lemon zest, 2 teaspoons minced fresh garlic, and $^1/_4$ teaspoon crushed red pepper in a food processor; process until finely ground, scraping sides as needed. With motor running, slowly add $^1/_2$ cup extra-virgin olive oil to kale mixture, processing until well blended, scraping sides as needed. Makes 1 $^3/_4$ cups

POULTRY

It's no secret that chicken is the most commonly used protein in any cook's weeknight repertoire, making it a challenge to think up interesting and tasty variations on the same theme night after night. Budget constraints make it even harder. Fear not. This chapter contains exciting new flavor combinations (as well as tasty twists on old standbys) that'll steer you far clear of a poultry rut.

Slow-Cooker Chicken with 40 Cloves of Garlic

Total cost $9.98

HANDS-ON 25 MIN.   TOTAL 8 HR., 25 MIN.   SERVES 4

There are about 10 cloves of garlic per head, so you'll need to purchase four whole heads for this recipe. If you don't grow your own fresh herbs, grab a package of poultry herbs from the produce section to substitute for the individual herbs. Add dried apricots to infuse the rich sauce with a fruity back note. Serve with couscous. Rehydrate ³/₄ cup in water according to package directions, fluff with a fork, and season to taste. Stir in dried apricots, if you like.

4 tablespoons melted butter, divided

40 peeled whole garlic cloves, divided

¹/₄ cup dried apricots, chopped

6 fresh thyme sprigs, plus more for garnish

1 fresh rosemary sprig

1 (3.5-pound) whole chicken

¹/₂ cup Overnight Chicken Stock (page 218) or store-bought

¹/₄ cup dry white wine

1 tablespoon all-purpose flour

1¹/₂ teaspoons chopped fresh thyme leaves, divided

2 tablespoons softened butter

2 teaspoons minced shallot

¹/₂ (8-ounce) baguette, sliced

1. Pour 3 tablespoons melted butter in a 6- or 7-quart slow cooker. Arrange 20 garlic cloves and apricots in a single layer in the slow cooker; add the thyme and rosemary sprigs. Place the chicken, breast side up, on top of the herbs. Brush with the remaining 1 tablespoon melted butter. Combine the stock and wine; pour over the chicken. Sprinkle the chicken generously with salt and pepper; arrange remaining garlic around the chicken. Cover and cook on LOW for 8 hours.

2. Carefully lift the chicken out of the slow cooker; place on a platter. Remove the garlic and apricots with a slotted spoon; set aside garlic and discard apricots. Strain the cooking liquid through a mesh strainer into a measuring cup; discard solids.

3. Place the flour in a small saucepan. Pour 1¹/₂ cups cooking liquid into the pan with the flour (reserve the remaining cooking liquid for another use), whisking until smooth. Set the pan over medium-high heat, and bring the sauce to a boil. Boil, whisking constantly, for 1 to 2 minutes or until thickened. Stir in 1 teaspoon chopped thyme, and season to taste with salt and pepper.

4. Meanwhile, arrange the top rack of the oven 5 inches from the broiler element. Preheat the broiler to high. Mash 6 reserved garlic cloves with the remaining ¹/₂ teaspoon thyme, the softened butter, and shallot. (Serve the remaining garlic cloves with the chicken or reserve for another use.) Spread 1 tablespoon of the garlic butter over the baguette slices (reserve the remaining garlic butter for another use), and arrange the bread in a single layer on a baking sheet. Broil for 2 to 3 minutes or until lightly browned. Serve the toast and sauce with the chicken. Garnish with thyme, if desired.

Pecan-Crusted Chicken & Cornmeal Waffles

Total cost $9.79

HANDS-ON **30 MIN.**   TOTAL **30 MIN.**   SERVES **4**

Get yourself organized before you start cooking, so the chicken is cooked just as you're turning out the waffles. Start by preheating your oven and waffle iron. Then measure all the ingredients and work on the chicken first. Once the chicken is in the oven, whip the waffle batter together and cook. Serve with Pineapple Tossed with Coconut on page 202.

3 tablespoons chopped toasted pecans

1 teaspoon fresh thyme leaves

$1/2$ cup panko breadcrumbs

2 tablespoons grated Parmesan

$1/2$ teaspoon garlic powder

$1/2$ teaspoon baking soda

$1/4$ teaspoon onion powder

$1/2$ cup all-purpose flour

$1/2$ cup buttermilk

1 large egg

2 (8-ounce) skinless, boneless chicken breast halves

$1^{1}/2$ teaspoons kosher salt, divided

$1^{1}/8$ teaspoons freshly ground black pepper, divided

2 tablespoons canola oil

Cornmeal Waffles

$3^{1}/2$ tablespoons agave nectar

$1^{1}/2$ tablespoons unsalted butter, melted

1 teaspoon fresh lemon juice

Pinch of salt

1. Preheat the oven to 425°F. Preheat a waffle iron to medium-high.

2. Place the pecans and thyme in a mini chopper; process until finely ground. Combine the pecan mixture, panko, and next 4 ingredients in a shallow dish. Place $1/2$ cup flour in a shallow dish. Whisk together the buttermilk and egg in another shallow dish.

3. Halve the chicken breasts horizontally to form 4 cutlets. Sprinkle with $1/2$ teaspoon salt and $1/4$ teaspoon pepper. Stir the remaining 1 teaspoon salt and $3/4$ teaspoon pepper into the pecan mixture. Dredge the cutlets in the flour; dip in the buttermilk mixture. Dredge in the pecan mixture, pressing to adhere.

4. Heat a large oven-safe skillet over medium-high heat. Add the oil to the pan; swirl to coat. Sauté the chicken for 3 minutes or until browned; turn chicken over. Place the pan in the oven, and bake at 425°F for 8 minutes or until the chicken is done.

5. Prepare the Cornmeal Waffles.

6. Whisk together the agave, melted butter, lemon juice, remaining $1/8$ teaspoon pepper, and a pinch of salt. Place 1 waffle on each of 4 plates; top each with 1 cutlet. Drizzle the agave mixture on top.

Cornmeal Waffles

Whisk together $1/4$ cup finely ground cornmeal, $1/4$ cup all-purpose flour, 1 teaspoon sugar, $1/2$ teaspoon baking powder, $1/4$ teaspoon kosher salt, and $1/8$ teaspoon baking soda. Combine $1/2$ cup room-temperature buttermilk, 2 tablespoons melted unsalted butter, and 1 room-temperature egg; add to cornmeal mixture. Whisk well. Coat a preheated waffle iron with cooking spray. Spoon about $1/4$ of the batter into the iron, and cook according to the manufacturer's directions to make 4 waffles.

Pimiento Cheese Chicken Breasts

Total cost $9.97

HANDS-ON **20 MIN.** TOTAL **37 MIN.** SERVES **4**

Stuffed chicken breasts seem a little retro, and it's time to revive the magic. Bring them into the modern age with a stuffing like pimiento cheese, spiked with a bit of bacon. Serve with Home Fries (page 199) and a simple salad. Halve $1/4$ cup grape tomatoes and thinly slice 3 radishes. Toss with 3 cups salad greens, 1 tablespoon fresh lemon juice, and 2 teaspoons olive oil. Season to taste with salt and pepper.

1 slice bacon

$3/4$ cup shredded sharp cheddar cheese

$2^1/2$ tablespoons mayonnaise

2 tablespoons minced green onions

$1^1/2$ tablespoons diced pimientos

2 teaspoons fresh lemon juice

$1/2$ teaspoon hot sauce

$3/4$ teaspoon salt, divided

4 (6-ounce) skinless, boneless chicken breast halves

$1/4$ teaspoon freshly ground black pepper

1 tablespoon canola oil

1. Preheat the oven to 350°F.

2. Cook the bacon in a large oven-safe skillet over medium heat until crisp, about 6 minutes. Remove the bacon, reserving the drippings in the pan; crumble the bacon. Combine the bacon, the next 6 ingredients, and $1/4$ teaspoon salt. Cut a 1-inch-wide slit into the thick end of each breast half; carefully cut down to the center of the chicken to form a deep pocket. Divide the cheese mixture evenly among the pockets. Secure the openings with wooden picks. Sprinkle the chicken with the remaining $1/2$ teaspoon salt and the pepper.

3. Heat the pan with the drippings over medium-high heat. Add the oil to the drippings; swirl. Add the chicken to the pan; cook 4 minutes. Turn the chicken over. Bake at 350°F for 12 minutes or until the chicken is done; let stand for 5 minutes before serving.

TIGHTWAD TIP
Chicken Breasts

Boneless, skinless chicken breasts are enormous these days. Save money by filleting two breast halves, horizontally, to make four reasonably sized portions.

Sautéed Chicken with Sage Browned Butter

Total cost $8.87

HANDS-ON **25 MIN.** TOTAL **25 MIN.** SERVES **4**

Dinner just doesn't get any easier than this delicious, superfast supper. Nutty browned butter is infused with the flavor of fresh sage, and the sauce is finished with fresh lemon, a tasty way to elevate an ordinary chicken breast. Serve with Cauliflower Rice (page 203) and Roasted Green Beans.

4 (6-ounce) skinless, boneless chicken breast halves

$3/4$ teaspoon salt

$1/4$ teaspoon freshly ground black pepper

$1/2$ cup all-purpose flour

1 tablespoon canola oil

$1/4$ cup unsalted butter

2 fresh sage sprigs

1 tablespoon minced shallot

1 teaspoon chopped fresh thyme

2 tablespoons fresh lemon juice

Sage Advice

One of my favorites, earthy sage, is the flavor of Thanksgiving to me. Maybe that's why it's often overshadowed by sister herbs basil and mint. Like most herbs, sage blooms in the warm temperatures of the spring and summer months, so there's no reason to wait until fall to incorporate some into your cooking. Use it in marinades and sauces for beef, pork, or chicken. When you grill, make a bundle of fresh sage, thyme, and rosemary sprigs, and use them in place of a pastry brush when basting meats or veggies.

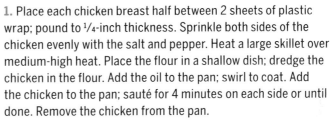

1. Place each chicken breast half between 2 sheets of plastic wrap; pound to $1/4$-inch thickness. Sprinkle both sides of the chicken evenly with the salt and pepper. Heat a large skillet over medium-high heat. Place the flour in a shallow dish; dredge the chicken in the flour. Add the oil to the pan; swirl to coat. Add the chicken to the pan; sauté for 4 minutes on each side or until done. Remove the chicken from the pan.

2. Add the butter and sage sprigs to the pan; cook over medium heat until the butter browns. Discard the sage. Add the shallot and thyme; cook for 30 seconds. Add the lemon juice; cook for 30 seconds. Serve with the chicken.

SERVE WITH
Roasted Green Beans

Preheat the oven to 425°F. Trim 1 pound fresh green beans or haricots verts (tiny French green beans), and toss with 1 tablespoon canola oil. Season to taste with salt and pepper. Roast at 425°F for 6 minutes. Add 2 tablespoons butter to the pan; toss the beans. Roast 2 to 4 more minutes or just until the beans are crisp-tender.

Lemon-Soy Grilled Chicken

Total cost $9.80

HANDS-ON **25 MIN.**   TOTAL **9 HR.**   SERVES **4**

Don't knock a mayo-based marinade until you try it. If this is your first, you're in for a wonderful treat. Before adding it to the chicken, set some aside to serve alongside the cooked chicken as a sauce. This is one of those recipes I just can't get enough of. Serve with Jicama & Bell Pepper Slaw on page 193, adding 2 cups of thinly sliced green cabbage.

1 cup mayonnaise

$1/2$ cup soy sauce

$1/2$ cup canola oil

6 tablespoons fresh lemon juice (about 2 lemons)

2 teaspoons sugar

4 chicken leg quarters (about 2 pounds)

1 teaspoon kosher salt

$1/2$ teaspoon freshly ground black pepper

1. Whisk together the first 5 ingredients. Set aside $1/2$ cup of the marinade to serve with the chicken. Place the chicken in a gallon-sized ziplock plastic bag; scrape the remaining marinade into the bag with the chicken. Seal the bag, and marinate in the refrigerator for 8 hours or overnight.

2. Prepare the grill for indirect grilling with half of the grill on medium-high heat and the other half of the grill on low. Remove the chicken from the bag; discard the marinade in the bag. Sprinkle the chicken evenly with the salt and pepper. Place the chicken, meaty side down, over medium-high heat; grill about 4 minutes to brown the chicken. Turn the chicken over, and place over low heat. Grill 20 to 25 minutes or until the chicken is done and a meat thermometer registers 160°F. Serve with the reserved $1/2$ cup sauce.

TIGHTWAD TIP
Chicken Leg Quarters

Although whole chickens are the least expensive per pound, if you have to buy already-cut parts, leg quarters are one of the best options. And they're adaptable to so many cooking techniques: grilling, stewing, braising, frying, or roasting.

Best Damn Chicken Pot Pie

Total cost $10.00

HANDS-ON **40 MIN.**   TOTAL **1 HR., 10 MIN.**   SERVES **4**

Keep the recipe for this pastry handy. First off, it's fantastic, but it's also easy to work with and very versatile. I use it all the time. Serve with Roasted Green Beans with Browned Butter (page 195) and corn muffins. Make half a batch of cornbread and bake in muffin tins.

FILLING

1 tablespoon canola oil

1 cup chopped onion

1/2 cup chopped carrot

1/4 cup chopped celery

4 skinless, boneless chicken thighs, chopped

1 teaspoon kosher salt

1/2 teaspoon black pepper

6 tablespoons all-purpose flour

2 fresh thyme sprigs

3 cups Overnight Chicken Stock (page 218) or store-bought

1 cup frozen green peas, thawed

2 green onions, thinly sliced

2 teaspoons chopped fresh thyme

Cooking spray

PASTRY

1 3/4 cups all-purpose flour (7.85 ounces)

6 tablespoons cornstarch

1/4 cup grated Parmesan cheese

3 tablespoons cornmeal

1 teaspoon kosher salt

1/4 teaspoon black pepper

1/2 cup cold butter, cut into small pieces

2 large egg yolks, divided

Ice-cold water

2 tablespoons heavy cream

1. Preheat the oven to 400°F.

2. To prepare the filling, heat the oil in a large saucepan over medium-high heat; swirl to coat. Add the onion, carrot, and celery; sauté for 4 minutes. Add the chicken, salt, and pepper; sauté 3 minutes. Stir in 6 tablespoons flour; cook 1 minute, stirring constantly. Add the thyme sprigs. Slowly pour the stock into the pan, stirring constantly; bring to a boil. Reduce the heat to medium; simmer 8 minutes, stirring occasionally. Remove from the heat. Discard the thyme sprigs. Stir in the peas, green onions, and chopped thyme. Pour the filling into a 9-inch pie plate or baking dish coated with cooking spray.

3. To prepare the pastry, weigh or lightly spoon the flour into dry measuring cups; level with a knife. Combine flour, cornstarch, Parmesan, cornmeal, salt, and pepper in the mixing bowl of a heavy-duty stand mixer with the paddle attachment. With the motor running at low speed, add the butter, 2 to 3 pieces at a time, beating until the butter breaks up into pea-sized pieces. Stir in 1 egg yolk. Add enough ice-cold water, 1 tablespoon at a time, until a moist dough forms, beating just until the dough forms a ball. Roll the dough out to a 12-inch circle. Place the dough over the top of the pie plate, folding the edges and fluting, pressing the edges into sides of pie plate to prevent them from sinking. Cut 3 to 5 slits in the top of the pastry to vent. If you want to be fancy, you can cut the dough into strips to create a lattice top.

4. Whisk together the cream and the remaining 1 egg yolk; brush the mixture over the top of the pastry. Bake at 400°F for 25 to 30 minutes or until the pastry is golden brown and cooked through.

Chicken Thighs with Cilantro Sauce

Total cost $8.40

HANDS-ON **20 MIN.**   TOTAL **20 MIN.**   SERVES **4**

This is an evergreen recipe that you can make all year-round, especially if you keep an herb garden. If not, visit your local Asian market to stock up on the ingredients. They should even have cilantro. Serve with Snap Pea Slaw on page 189 and 2 cups hot cooked rice.

Cooking spray

8 bone-in, skin-on chicken thighs

1¼ teaspoons kosher salt, divided

2 tablespoons finely chopped shallot

1 large garlic clove, minced

⅓ cup finely chopped fresh cilantro

1½ tablespoons dark sesame oil

1 tablespoon lower-sodium soy sauce

½ teaspoon sambal oelek (ground fresh chile paste)

½ teaspoon grated fresh lime zest

1. Heat a large skillet over medium-high heat. Coat the pan with cooking spray. Sprinkle the chicken evenly with 1 teaspoon salt. Add the chicken to the pan, skin side down; cook for 6 minutes or until browned. Turn over, and reduce heat to medium. Cook chicken for 10 to 12 minutes or until the chicken is done. Place the chicken on a platter.

2. Place the remaining ¼ teaspoon salt, shallot, and garlic in a small food processor; process until finely chopped, scraping sides as needed. Add the cilantro to the garlic mixture in the processor; pulse to combine. With the motor running, add the oil and remaining ingredients to the cilantro mixture in mini chopper; process until a fine paste forms. Serve the cilantro mixture with the chicken.

TIGHTWAD TIP
Cilantro

I've never had much luck growing cilantro, so I buy it at the Hispanic market, where it's three bunches for $0.99 (or $0.33 per bunch). It's also inexpensive at the Asian market.

Braised Chicken with Blistered Plums

Total cost $9.05

HANDS-ON **40 MIN.**   TOTAL **45 MIN.**   SERVES **4**

Although the recipe is written for the stovetop and broiler, you can easily take this gem out to the grill. Just sear the chicken on the grill, use an oven-safe pot (such as cast iron) with a lid, and braise the chicken in the pot on the grill. Instead of broiling the plums, you can easily grill them too. If you want to give this recipe a whirl on the grill, keep an even medium heat of about 350°F and be aware that your cook times may vary. While the chicken cooks, steam or simmer 2 cups rice to serve alongside.

1 teaspoon salt, divided

³/₄ teaspoon freshly ground black pepper, divided

1 teaspoon brown sugar

¹/₈ teaspoon ground cinnamon

8 bone-in, skin-on chicken thighs

¹/₄ cup butter, divided

4 teaspoons extra-virgin olive oil, divided

1 cup thinly diagonally sliced red onion

2 garlic cloves, minced

¹/₄ cup brandy

1 cup Overnight Chicken Stock (page 218) or store-bought

¹/₂ teaspoon dried rubbed sage

4 small ripe plums, pitted and halved

2 tablespoons fresh lemon juice, divided

2 teaspoons honey

¹/₂ teaspoon chopped fresh thyme leaves

1 green onion, thinly diagonally sliced

1. Combine ⁵/₈ teaspoon salt, ¹/₄ teaspoon pepper, sugar, and cinnamon, stirring well; sprinkle over both sides of the chicken.

2. Melt 2 tablespoons butter in a large skillet over medium-high heat. Add 4 chicken thighs to the pan, skin side down; cook 4 minutes or until golden brown. Turn the chicken thighs over; cook 2 minutes. Remove the chicken from the pan. Repeat the procedure with the remaining 2 tablespoons butter and 4 chicken thighs.

3. Add 1 tablespoon oil to the pan; swirl to coat. Add the sliced red onion; sauté 2 minutes, stirring frequently. Add the garlic; sauté 1 minute, stirring constantly. Remove the pan from the heat; stir in the brandy. Return the pan to the heat; cook 1 minute or until the liquid evaporates. Stir in ¹/₄ teaspoon salt, ¹/₄ teaspoon pepper, stock, and sage; bring to a boil. Return the chicken to the pan, skin side up. Cover, reduce the heat to low, and simmer about 18 minutes or until the chicken is done.

4. While the chicken cooks, arrange the top rack of the oven 5 inches from the broiler element. Preheat the broiler to high. Arrange the plums, cut sides up, on a sturdy, foil-lined baking sheet. Combine remaining 1 teaspoon oil, 1 tablespoon lemon juice, and honey; brush the mixture over the plums. Sprinkle with the remaining ¹/₈ teaspoon salt. Broil 3 to 4 minutes or until slightly charred; sprinkle with the thyme.

5. Place 2 plum halves and 2 chicken thighs on each of 4 plates. Stir the remaining 1 tablespoon lemon juice into the onion mixture. Adjust the seasoning as needed; sprinkle with the green onion. Serve the sauce with the chicken and plums.

Moroccan Chicken Skewers

Total cost
$9.47

HANDS-ON **10 MIN.**   TOTAL **2 HR., 10 MIN.**   SERVES **4**

Serve with Roasted Cauliflower and Couscous Pilaf or serve with plain cooked couscous, if preferred. Give the couscous nutty flavor by toasting it in a hot pan before you rehydrate it, if you like.

2 tablespoons olive oil

1½ tablespoons minced fresh garlic

1½ tablespoons sambal oelek (ground fresh chile paste)

1 teaspoon ground cumin

½ teaspoon grated fresh lemon zest

⅛ teaspoon ground cinnamon

1 teaspoon kosher salt, divided

8 skinless, boneless chicken thighs, cut into 36 pieces

12 cherry tomatoes

1 small red onion, cut into 12 wedges

1 yellow bell pepper, cut into 12 pieces

Cooking spray

½ cup plain Greek yogurt

Roasted Cauliflower

Preheat the oven to 450°F. Place a small roasting pan in the oven while it preheats. Toss 4 cups cauliflower florets with 2 tablespoons canola oil; sprinkle with salt and pepper. Arrange the cauliflower in preheated pan, cut sides down; roast at 450°F for 18 minutes. Stir 1 tablespoon butter into the cauliflower mixture. Roast 5 to 8 more minutes or until the butter browns and the cauliflower is well roasted.

1. Combine the first 6 ingredients in a small mixing bowl; stir in ¼ teaspoon salt. Scrape the mixture into a ziplock plastic bag. Add the chicken to the bag. Seal the bag, and marinate in the refrigerator for 2 hours, turning after 1 hour.

2. Meanwhile, immerse 12 (8-inch) wooden skewers in water; soak 30 minutes. Drain and pat dry.

3. Preheat the grill to medium-high heat.

4. Remove the chicken from the marinade; discard marinade. Thread 3 chicken pieces, 1 tomato, 1 onion wedge, and 1 pepper piece alternately onto each skewer, beginning and ending with chicken; sprinkle evenly with the remaining ¾ teaspoon salt. Arrange the skewers on a grill rack coated with cooking spray; grill 4 to 5 minutes on each side or until the chicken is done. Serve with the yogurt.

SERVE WITH
Couscous Pilaf

Cook 1 cup dry couscous according to the package directions, using equal parts Overnight Chicken Stock (page 218) or store-bought stock and orange juice for the cooking liquid. Toss ⅓ cup dried cherries and 3 thinly sliced green onions with the hot cooked couscous.

Total cost $6.64

HOW LOW CAN YOU GO?!

Chicken & Brown Rice Bake

HANDS-ON 15 MIN.   TOTAL 38 MIN.   SERVES 4

If you ever find leftover rice kicking around, make this recipe to use it up. I love the texture of chewy brown rice in the mix, but any cooked rice will work. Serve it with a half recipe of Grissini on page 226. If you need to cook brown rice, start the Grissini while you wait for the rice to simmer and cool.

1 cup uncooked brown rice

2 teaspoons canola oil

2 skinless, boneless chicken thighs

1 teaspoon kosher salt

³/₄ teaspoon pepper

3 tablespoons unsalted butter, divided

1 (8-ounce) package frozen artichoke hearts, thawed

2 teaspoons minced fresh garlic

2 tablespoons all-purpose flour

1 cup whole milk

¹/₂ cup Overnight Chicken Stock (page 218) or store-bought

¹/₂ cup shredded Swiss cheese

2 tablespoons mayonnaise

2 cups fresh baby spinach

1 teaspoon grated fresh lemon zest

1 tablespoon fresh lemon juice

Cooking spray

¹/₂ cup Bacon & Chive Breadcrumbs (page 225)

1. Cook the rice according to the package directions.

2. Preheat the oven to 450°F.

3. Heat a small sauté pan over medium-high heat. Add the oil to the pan; swirl to coat. Sprinkle the chicken with the salt and pepper. Sauté the chicken for 5 minutes on each side or until done. Cool chicken for 5 minutes; chop.

4. Melt 1 tablespoon butter in a small saucepan over medium-high heat. Add the artichokes; cook 2 minutes, stirring occasionally. Stir in the garlic; cook 30 seconds, stirring constantly. Scrape the artichoke mixture into a large bowl; return the pan to the heat. Melt the remaining 2 tablespoons butter. Add the flour; sauté 1 minute, whisking constantly. Slowly add the milk and stock, whisking constantly. Bring the mixture to a boil; cook 3 minutes or until thickened. Remove from the heat; let stand 5 minutes. Add the cheese and mayonnaise; whisk until smooth. Season to taste with salt and pepper.

5. Add the rice, chopped chicken, and sauce to the bowl with the artichoke mixture; stir to combine. Stir in the spinach, lemon zest, and lemon juice. Season to taste with salt and pepper; stir well. Scrape the mixture into an 11- x 7-inch baking dish coated with cooking spray; top with the breadcrumbs. Bake at 450°F for 18 to 20 minutes or until browned and bubbly.

Frozen Artichoke Hearts

If you've never tried frozen artichoke hearts, you need to go get some. Right now. All canned and jarred products—even ones that don't have a dreadful marinade—have issues with flavor and texture. The frozen product is the closest thing to fresh that you'll find, and you don't have to slave over peeling and cleaning them.

Maple-Mustard Chicken Thighs

Total cost $9.97

HANDS-ON **15 MIN.**   TOTAL **2 HR., 31 MIN.**   SERVES **4**

If you're pressed for time, you can marinate the chicken in as few as 30 minutes since you'll reserve some of the mustard mixture to sauce the cooked chicken. Serve with Easy Slaw and Potato Salad. Mix some red cabbage into the slaw for added color.

$\frac{1}{3}$ cup spicy brown mustard

2 tablespoons brown sugar

3 tablespoons maple syrup

2 tablespoons yellow mustard

1 tablespoon grated onion

1 tablespoon cider vinegar

2 teaspoons lower-sodium soy sauce

$\frac{1}{2}$ teaspoon black pepper

1 garlic clove, minced

8 bone-in chicken thighs, skinned

$\frac{1}{2}$ teaspoon kosher salt

Cooking spray

1. Combine the first 9 ingredients in a bowl. Place half of the mixture in a ziplock plastic bag; set remaining mixture aside. Add the chicken to bag. Seal the bag, and marinate in the refrigerator for 2 hours.

2. Preheat the grill to medium-high heat.

3. Remove the chicken from the bag. Sprinkle the chicken with the salt. Place the chicken on a grill rack coated with cooking spray; grill 8 minutes on each side or until done. Serve with the reserved mustard mixture.

SERVE WITH

Easy Slaw

Combine 4 cups green cabbage, $\frac{1}{4}$ cup thinly sliced red onion, and 1 medium carrot, shredded. Drizzle with 2 tablespoons extra-virgin olive oil, 1 tablespoon cider vinegar, and 1 tablespoon fresh lemon juice. Toss with 1 teaspoon kosher salt, $\frac{1}{2}$ teaspoon sugar, and $\frac{1}{4}$ teaspoon freshly ground black pepper.

Potato Salad

Quarter 1 pound of small red-skinned potatoes. Place potatoes in a saucepan; cover with water to a depth of 2 inches above potatoes. Bring water to a boil over medium-high heat; boil for 6 to 10 minutes or until potatoes are tender. Drain; rinse potatoes with cool water. Drain. Place potatoes in a bowl; season to taste with salt and pepper. Add 2 thinly sliced green onions. Whisk together $\frac{1}{2}$ cup mayonnaise and $\frac{1}{4}$ cup sour cream. Add to potatoes; toss. Stir in 2 tablespoons fresh lemon juice. Adjust the seasoning as needed. Chill until ready to serve.

Stuffed Sweet Potatoes

Total cost $8.61

HANDS-ON **20 MIN.**   TOTAL **48 MIN.**   SERVES **4**

Twice-baked potatoes are always a crowd-pleaser. So why not do a twist with sweet potatoes? This recipe is as easy as it is delicious. Pair it with A Big Salad.

2 large sweet potatoes

2 teaspoons canola oil

2 skinless, boneless chicken thighs

$^3/_4$ teaspoon kosher salt, divided

$^3/_4$ teaspoon freshly ground black pepper, divided

$^3/_4$ cup chopped broccoli florets

$^1/_3$ cup Alabama-Style White BBQ Sauce (page 222)

3 tablespoons finely chopped red onion

2 teaspoons fresh lemon juice

2 slices applewood-smoked bacon, cooked and crumbled

$^1/_2$ cup grated Parmesan cheese, divided

TIGHTWAD TIP
Make It a Side

Omit the chicken from these potatoes for a tasty and versatile side to serve with grilled pork or chicken.

1. Preheat the oven to 425°F.

2. Prick the potatoes all over with a fork, and place on a microwave-safe plate. Microwave on HIGH just until tender, 8 to 10 minutes, turning halfway through. Cool the potatoes for 20 minutes. Halve the potatoes lengthwise, and scoop out the pulp, leaving a $^1/_4$-inch-thick border around the edges. Place the potato pulp in a medium mixing bowl.

3. Meanwhile, heat a small sauté pan over medium-high heat. Add the oil; swirl to coat. Sprinkle the chicken with $^1/_2$ teaspoon each of salt and pepper; add to the pan. Cook for 5 to 6 minutes on each side or until done. Let rest for 5 minutes; chop.

4. Cook the broccoli in boiling salted water for 2 minutes or just until crisp-tender; drain. Rinse the broccoli with cold running water for about 1 minute. Pat dry.

5. Add the chopped chicken, blanched broccoli, BBQ sauce, and the next 3 ingredients to the bowl with the sweet potato pulp. Add $^1/_4$ cup cheese to the chicken mixture, season with the remaining $^1/_4$ teaspoon each of salt and pepper, and stir to combine. Divide the chicken mixture evenly among the potato shells; top each shell with 1 tablespoon cheese.

6. Place the potatoes on a foil-lined baking sheet. Bake at 425°F for 20 minutes or until lightly browned and heated through.

SERVE WITH
A Big Salad

Place 4 cups torn romaine lettuce in a large salad bowl. Top with 2 cups baby spinach, 1 cup shaved carrot, and $^1/_4$ cup thinly sliced red onion. Sprinkle with salt and pepper. Whisk together 2 tablespoons cider vinegar, 1 teaspoon honey, 1 teaspoon Dijon mustard, and 3 tablespoons extra-virgin olive oil; toss with the salad. Sprinkle $^1/_4$ cup chopped toasted pecans over the salad. Serve immediately.

Fiery Chicken Thighs with Crispy Yogurt Rice

Total cost $8.63

HANDS-ON **40 MIN.**   TOTAL **1 HR.**   SERVES **4**

Pay close attention to the rice as it cooks over medium-low heat—when you hear it begin to crackle, turn the heat down to low. Continue to cook until the bottom side of the rice develops a golden crust. Serve with 1 pound fresh green beans sautéed in 2 tablespoons butter; toss with 3 tablespoons toasted sliced almonds. Although the buttery rice cuts through the heat of the chicken, use less chile paste if you are not a fan of spicy foods.

³/₄ cup long-grain white rice

2¹/₂ tablespoons canola oil, divided

1¹/₂ teaspoons ground cumin, divided

1 tablespoon sambal oelek (ground fresh chile paste)

1 tablespoon minced fresh garlic

¹/₄ teaspoon ground coriander

4 bone-in, skin-on chicken thighs

1 teaspoon kosher salt, divided

³/₄ cup chopped onion

¹/₂ teaspoon ground turmeric

¹/₂ cup plain 2% reduced-fat Greek yogurt

1¹/₂ tablespoons butter

Cooking spray

1. Bring 5 cups water to a boil in medium saucepan. Add the rice; boil 10 minutes. Drain. Rinse rice; drain.

2. Combine 1 tablespoon oil, ¹/₂ teaspoon cumin, sambal oelek, garlic, and coriander in a small bowl, stirring well. Scrape spice paste into a zip-top plastic bag. Add chicken to bag; seal. Toss to coat. Let stand 20 minutes. Remove chicken from bag; discard marinade. Sprinkle chicken evenly with ¹/₄ teaspoon salt.

3. Heat a medium, heavy-bottomed skillet over medium heat. Add 1¹/₂ teaspoons oil to the pan; swirl to coat. Add the onion; cook 5 minutes. Stir in remaining 1 teaspoon cumin, remaining ³/₄ teaspoon salt, and turmeric; cook 1 minute. Combine rice, onion mixture, and yogurt in a bowl.

4. Return pan to medium-high heat. Add the butter and remaining 1 tablespoon oil to pan; swirl until butter melts. Add rice mixture to pan, lightly packing rice down. Reduce heat to medium-low. Wrap a clean, dry dish towel around the lid, tying it at the handle; place prepared lid on pan. Cook rice, covered, over medium-low heat 10 minutes (do not stir or uncover). Reduce temperature to low; cook 20 more minutes or until rice is tender on top and a golden crust forms on bottom.

5. Loosen the rice crust with a rubber spatula around the edges. Place a plate over the top of pan, and invert the rice onto plate, browned side up.

6. Arrange the top rack of the oven 10 inches from the broiler element. While rice cooks, preheat the broiler to high.

7. Place chicken, skin-side up, on a foil-lined broiler pan coated with cooking spray. Broil 8 minutes or until browned. Turn chicken over; broil 4 more minutes or until done. Serve with rice.

Southwest Chicken & Quinoa Bowls

Total cost
$6.92

HANDS-ON 25 MIN.   TOTAL 45 MIN.   SERVES 4

These bowls are healthy, colorful, and full of flavor. Chicken thighs vary in size, so if you get small ones, they may cook a little faster than the big ones I used in testing. It's always better to err on the side of caution, which is not a problem with chicken thighs because they're very forgiving.

³/₄ cup uncooked quinoa

1¹/₄ teaspoons kosher salt, divided

³/₄ teaspoon ground cumin

¹/₄ teaspoon smoked paprika

¹/₄ teaspoon garlic powder

4 bone-in, skin-on chicken thighs

2¹/₂ tablespoons canola oil, divided

1¹/₂ teaspoons sugar

1 (12-ounce) sweet potato, peeled and cut into ¹/₂-inch cubes

1 (15.5-ounce) can black beans, drained and rinsed

1 cup chopped tomato

1¹/₂ teaspoons minced fresh garlic

¹/₂ teaspoon grated fresh lemon zest

3 green onions, thinly vertically sliced

¹/₂ cup Avocado-Ranch Dressing (page 214)

2 (6-inch) pitas, cut in wedges and toasted

1. Preheat the oven to 400°F.

2. Cook the quinoa in boiling salted water for 15 minutes; drain. Combine 1 teaspoon salt and the next 3 ingredients, stirring well. Sprinkle 1¹/₄ teaspoons seasoning blend over both sides of the chicken. Heat a large oven-safe sauté pan over medium-high heat. Add 1 tablespoon oil to the pan; swirl to coat. Add the chicken to pan, skin side down, and cook until the skin is golden brown and crisp, about 4 minutes. Turn the chicken over; cook until golden brown, about 4 minutes. Place the pan in the oven. Bake at 400°F for 10 to 12 minutes or until the chicken is done. Let stand 5 minutes. Remove the chicken from the bones; chop. Discard the bones (or reserve for stock).

3. Stir the sugar into the remaining spice blend. Toss the sweet potato with 1 tablespoon oil. Sprinkle the sweet potato mixture with the sugar-spice blend. Spread the sweet potato mixture in a single layer on a baking sheet; roast at 400°F for about 18 minutes or until tender and golden, stirring potatoes after 12 minutes. Toss the sweet potatoes with the beans. Toss the tomato with the garlic, zest, and remaining 1¹/₂ teaspoons oil. Sprinkle with the remaining ¹/₄ teaspoon salt; toss.

4. Divide the quinoa among 4 bowls. Arrange ¹/₄ of the sweet potato mixture atop each serving. Spoon ¹/₄ of the tomato mixture beside the sweet potato mixture; place ¹/₄ of the chicken next to the tomato mixture. Sprinkle with the green onions, and serve with the dressing and pita.

Sticky Chicken Drumsticks

Total cost $8.15

HANDS-ON 15 MIN. **TOTAL** 45 MIN. **SERVES** 4

Drumsticks are not only affordable, they're fun. Kids, big and little, love to eat with their hands. With this glaze, things will get a little messy, but the flavor is well worth the extra napkins. Serve with Tropical Cabbage Crunch Slaw on page 190.

1 large lime

3 tablespoons brown sugar

2 tablespoons honey

2 tablespoons soy sauce

2 tablespoons minced fresh garlic

1 tablespoon unseasoned rice vinegar

1 teaspoon sambal oelek (ground fresh chile paste)

1 teaspoon toasted sesame oil

Cooking spray

8 chicken drumsticks (about 2½ pounds)

1 teaspoon kosher salt

½ teaspoon freshly ground black pepper

3 green onions, thinly diagonally sliced

1. Preheat the oven to 400°F.

2. Grate ¼ teaspoon zest from the lime into a small bowl. Squeeze 3 tablespoons juice from the lime into a small saucepan. Add the brown sugar and the next 5 ingredients to the saucepan with juice; bring to a boil over medium-high heat, stirring just until the sugar dissolves, about 1 minute. Reduce the heat to medium, and simmer 2 minutes or just until the mixture thickens to a syrupy consistency. Remove from the heat, and stir in the sesame oil. Remove 3 tablespoons glaze to a small bowl. Stir the zest into the reserved glaze; keep warm and set aside.

3. Line a baking sheet with foil; coat the foil with cooking spray. Place the chicken in a single layer on the prepared pan, and season with salt and pepper. Toss the chicken with reserved 3 tablespoons glaze.

4. Bake at 400°F for 15 minutes. Turn the chicken over; brush with the remaining glaze, and bake for 10 to 12 more minutes or until a meat thermometer registers 165°F. Place the chicken on a platter. Sprinkle with the green onions.

Mediterranean Stuffed Spaghetti Squash

Total cost $8.97

HANDS-ON 25 MIN. TOTAL 1 HR., 15 MIN. SERVES 4

Spaghetti squash vary in size. I always search out the small to medium ones for this recipe—any bigger and they're just unwieldy. After the squash roast, halve them, scrape out the seeds, and scoop this awesome filling into the center of each half. A few words of advice: The squash will explode in the oven if you don't prick them before you put them in to cook. Trust me. Not fun. Also, after you scrape the seeds out of each half, season the squash with a dash of salt and pepper and maybe even a drizzle of olive oil, since your "bowl" is edible.

2 small spaghetti squash

1³/₄ teaspoons kosher salt, divided

¹/₂ teaspoon black pepper

2¹/₂ tablespoons extra-virgin olive oil, divided

³/₄ cup finely chopped yellow onion

1 medium carrot, peeled and diced (about ³/₄ cup)

12 ounces lean ground turkey

¹/₂ teaspoon ground cinnamon

¹/₂ teaspoon ground cumin

¹/₄ teaspoon smoked paprika

¹/₈ teaspoon ground dried ginger

Pinch of crushed red pepper

²/₃ cup All-Purpose Tomato Sauce (page 221)

3 tablespoons dried cherries

2 teaspoons honey

¹/₃ cup crumbled feta cheese

¹/₄ cup pitted kalamata olives, halved

3 green onions, thinly sliced

¹/₄ cup grated Parmesan cheese

2 tablespoons chopped fresh chives

1. Preheat the oven to 400°F.

2. Pierce the whole squash with a fork; place on a baking sheet. Bake at 400°F for 1 hour or until the squash are tender. Cool 30 minutes. Halve the squashes lengthwise; discard the seeds. Sprinkle the squash halves evenly with 1 teaspoon salt and the pepper, and drizzle with 1 tablespoon oil.

3. Meanwhile, heat a medium skillet over medium-high heat. Add the remaining 1¹/₂ tablespoons oil to the pan; swirl to coat. Add the onion and carrot, and cook, stirring occasionally, for 3 to 4 minutes or until starting to soften. Add the turkey and the next 5 ingredients; sauté 6 to 8 minutes or until turkey is browned, stirring to crumble.

4. Add the remaining ³/₄ teaspoon salt, tomato sauce, cherries, and honey, and bring to a boil. Remove from the heat. Stir in the feta, olives, and green onions. Adjust the salt and pepper as needed. Divide the mixture evenly among the squash halves. Sprinkle each serving with the Parmesan.

5. Arrange the top rack of the oven 8 inches from the broiler element. Preheat the broiler to high. Arrange the stuffed squash on a baking sheet; broil 3 to 5 minutes or until lightly browned and heated. Sprinkle the squash with the chives before serving.

Turkey-Bacon-Cheddar Meatloaf

Total cost $9.49

HANDS-ON 20 MIN.   TOTAL 1 HR., 10 MIN.   SERVES 4

Ground turkey isn't very forgiving, and it can dry out easily. When you add bacon, cheese, and Alabama-Style White BBQ Sauce to the meatloaf mixture before it's cooked, the results are moist and delicious. If you have a mini food processor, use it to process the uncooked bacon, which is tricky to chop by hand unless you have a razor-sharp knife. Serve with Mashed Red Potatoes. Prepare Easy Smashed Potatoes (page 115), substituting red-skinned potatoes for Yukon Gold.

2 teaspoons canola oil

$1/2$ cup finely chopped carrot

$1/2$ cup shredded sharp cheddar cheese, divided

$1/3$ cup plus 2 tablespoons Alabama-Style White BBQ Sauce (page 222)

$1/2$ teaspoon kosher salt

$1/8$ teaspoon freshly ground black pepper

3 green onions, thinly diagonally sliced

2 slices applewood-smoked bacon, finely chopped

1 (20.8-ounce) package lean ground turkey

1 large egg

Cooking spray

1. Preheat the oven to 375°F.

2. Heat a small sauté pan over medium-high heat. Add the oil to the pan; swirl to coat. Add the carrot, and sauté for 2 to 3 minutes or just until lightly browned. Transfer the carrot to a large mixing bowl. Add $1/4$ cup cheese, $1/3$ cup BBQ sauce, and the next 4 ingredients to the bowl with the carrot; toss. Add the turkey and egg, and mix gently just until combined.

3. Scrape the turkey mixture into an 8- x 4-inch loaf pan coated with cooking spray. Bake at 375°F for 30 minutes. Remove the pan, and increase the oven temperature to 450°F.

4. Spread the remaining 2 tablespoons BBQ sauce over the top of the meatloaf, and sprinkle with the remaining $1/4$ cup cheese. Bake at 450°F for 10 to 15 minutes or until done and a meat thermometer registers 160°F. Let stand at room temperature at least 10 minutes. Cut into 8 slices.

Sausage, Mushroom & Potato Gratin

Total cost $9.86

HANDS-ON **35 MIN.**   TOTAL **1 HR., 20 MIN.**   SERVES **4**

Home fries meet casserole in this ultimate comfort food that's great for brunch or dinner. Fans of fiery flavors: Use hot Italian or turkey Italian sausage. Although red-skinned potatoes add color, you can use russet potatoes if you have them on hand. Serve with Citrus Fruit Salad.

1 tablespoon extra-virgin olive oil

2 (4-ounce) turkey Italian sausage links, casings removed

2 tablespoons butter

3 cups chopped onion

4 ounces sliced cremini mushrooms

1½ pounds red-skinned potatoes, coarsely chopped

1 teaspoon kosher salt

¼ teaspoon freshly ground black pepper

⅛ teaspoon crushed red pepper

½ cup Overnight Chicken Stock (page 218) or store-bought

Cooking spray

¾ cup shredded Swiss cheese (3 ounces)

1 tablespoon chopped fresh chives

TIGHTWAD TIP
Buying Cheese

It's always most economical to buy a block of cheese and shred it yourself. Shred just as much as you need, so the flavor stays fresh.

1. Preheat the oven to 400°F.

2. Heat a large sauté pan over medium-high heat. Add the oil to the pan; swirl to coat. Add the sausage to the pan; sauté for 5 minutes or until browned, stirring to crumble. Remove the sausage from the pan, reserving the drippings in the pan. Melt the butter in the drippings in the pan. Add the onion; cook 6 minutes, stirring occasionally. Add the mushrooms; cook 6 minutes, stirring occasionally. Add the potatoes, salt, and peppers; cook 8 minutes or until browned, stirring occasionally.

3. Stir in the sausage and stock. Remove from the heat. Spoon the potato mixture into an 11- x 7-inch baking dish coated with cooking spray; top with the cheese. Cover and bake at 400°F for 30 minutes. Uncover and bake 15 more minutes or until golden. Sprinkle with the chives.

SERVE WITH
Citrus Fruit Salad

Section 2 oranges and 1 Ruby Red grapefruit, holding the fruit over a small bowl to capture the juices as you work. Place the segments in a medium mixing bowl. Quarter and core 1 red-skinned apple, leaving the peel on; slice. Add 1 tablespoon fresh lemon juice to the bowl with the orange and grapefruit juices. Toss the apple slices with the citrus juices. Sprinkle with 2 tablespoons sugar; toss. Stir the apple mixture into the orange mixture; toss.

MEATS

Meats like beef, pork, and lamb pose a challenge for budget-minded cooks: Many people consider a meal incomplete without them, though they're often the most expensive ingredients per pound on the plate—when you buy the premium steak and chop cuts. And that's where most folks go wrong. Fact is, the cheaper cuts are almost always more flavorful. When you cook them right (the tougher stuff needs to go low and slow), they're every bit as tender and juicy as the pricey portions. And when you think of meat not as the star of the meal but rather a supporting player, you turn out supremely satisfying meals where your dollar goes further.

Beer-Braised Beef with Onions, Carrots & Turnips

Total cost $8.78

HANDS-ON **30 MIN.**   TOTAL **3 HR., 35 MIN.**   SERVES **4**

Making this recipe with a dark beer adds a wonderfully deep, rich flavor. You can take a more traditional route and use red wine instead, if you prefer. Slice your red onion, prepare the baking sheet, and have it all ready to go into the oven during the last 10 minutes the beef cooks. Pair this with Slow-Cooker Grits on page 203 to round out the meal.

1 (1-pound) boneless chuck roast

1³/₄ teaspoons salt, divided

¹/₂ teaspoon black pepper

¹/₄ cup all-purpose flour, divided

2 tablespoons canola oil

1 cup Overnight Chicken Stock (page 218) or store-bought

8 garlic cloves, crushed

1 (12-ounce) bottle dark beer

1 medium-sized yellow onion, halved

1 bay leaf

3 carrots, peeled and cut diagonally into ¹/₂-inch-thick slices

8 ounces small turnips, cut into wedges

1 medium-sized red onion, cut into ¹/₄-inch-thick slices

2 teaspoons olive oil

2 tablespoons butter

2 tablespoons chopped fresh flat-leaf parsley

3 cups Slow-Cooker Grits (page 203)

1. Preheat the oven to 300°F.

2. Heat a Dutch oven over medium-high. Sprinkle the beef on all sides with 1¹/₄ teaspoons salt and pepper, and rub with 3 tablespoons flour. Add the canola oil to the pan; swirl to coat. Add the beef to the pan; cook 10 minutes, turning to brown on all sides. Add the stock and the next 4 ingredients, scraping the pan to release the browned bits; bring to a boil. Cover and bake at 300°F for 1¹/₂ hours. Add the carrots; cover and cook for 25 minutes. Add the remaining ¹/₂ teaspoon salt and turnips; cover and cook for 1 hour and 5 more minutes or until the vegetables are tender and the beef is fork-tender.

3. Arrange the top rack of the oven 5 inches from the broiler element. Preheat the broiler to high.

4. Arrange the red onion on a lightly greased foil-lined baking sheet; brush with the olive oil. Sprinkle lightly with salt and pepper. Broil 3 to 5 minutes or until charred.

5. Remove and reserve the beef, carrots, and turnips to a serving bowl; discard the yellow onion and bay leaf. Skim the pan juices with a spoon, if desired. Melt the butter in a small saucepan over medium-high heat. Whisk in the remaining 1 tablespoon flour; cook 1 minute, whisking often. Gradually add the pan juices, whisking constantly; cook about 1 minute or until the sauce is smooth and thickened slightly. Add the red onion to the beef mixture and adjust seasoning as needed; sprinkle with the parsley. Serve with the sauce and Slow-Cooker Grits.

 TIGHTWAD TIP Chuck Roast

Ask your butcher to cut a 1-pound roast for you, or buy a larger one (especially if it's on sale), cut off a pound yourself, and wrap and freeze the rest for later.

Sheet Pan Steak with Blistered Veggies

Total cost $9.00

HANDS-ON **24 MIN.**   TOTAL **33 MIN.**   SERVES **4**

If you can't find a flap steak, look for a sirloin steak. Sirloin tip roast will do in a pinch—ask your butcher to cut you a steak. Like flank, flap steak can get tough and chewy if cooked much beyond medium. Sometimes this cut is thick and other times it's thinner, which means it'll cook more quickly. It's always a good idea to check for doneness early, because it'll continue cooking even after you pull it from the oven.

1 small red onion, cut into wedges

Cooking spray

3 tablespoons canola oil, divided

Kosher salt

Freshly ground black pepper

1 (1½-pound) beef flap steak, trimmed

8 ounces fresh broccoli florets

2 cups fresh cauliflower florets

1 pound fresh haricots verts (tiny French green beans), trimmed

2 tablespoons butter, softened

2 teaspoons chopped fresh flat-leaf parsley

1 teaspoon minced shallot

½ teaspoon grated fresh lemon zest

¼ teaspoon salt

1 small garlic clove, minced

 TIGHTWAD TIP
Budget-Friendly Cuts

Sometimes called flap meat, sirloin tip steak is a lean cut, similar to flank steak but less expensive.

1. Preheat the oven to 400°F.

2. Arrange the onion on one end of a baking sheet lightly coated with cooking spray; drizzle with 1 teaspoon oil. Sprinkle with the salt and pepper. Bake at 400°F for 5 minutes. Season the steak with salt and pepper, and drizzle with 1 tablespoon oil. Toss the broccoli and cauliflower with 1 tablespoon oil; sprinkle with salt and pepper. Arrange the steak, cauliflower, and broccoli in a single layer on the baking sheet with the onion. Bake at 400°F for 8 minutes. Remove pan from oven.

3. Arrange the top rack of the oven 5 inches from the broiler element. Preheat the broiler to high.

4. Toss the beans with 1 teaspoon oil; season with salt and pepper. Arrange the beans on the baking sheet with the steak and vegetables. Broil 7 minutes or until the steak and vegetables are charred and a meat thermometer registers the steak at 135°F (for medium-rare) or until desired degree of doneness. Remove the steak from baking sheet; let stand at room temperature for 6 to 8 minutes before slicing. Thinly slice across the grain.

5. Meanwhile, stir together the remaining 1 teaspoon oil, butter, parsley, shallot, lemon zest, ¼ teaspoon salt, and garlic. Place the butter on the hot steak to melt as it rests; brush evenly over the steak. Serve with the vegetables.

Korean-Style Beef Tacos

Total cost $9.68

HANDS-ON: **30 MIN.**   TOTAL **1 HR., 30 MIN.**   SERVES **4**

Slice the steak before you marinate it, so the flavor will fully permeate every bite. Once you get the steak in the fridge, go ahead and make the Quick-Pickled Cabbage and start the Sesame Rice about 15 minutes before you're ready to grill. That way everything will be ready all at the same time. Be sure to look for unseasoned rice vinegar so you know that there's no added sugar or salt. If using wooden skewers, be sure to soak them in water for at least 30 minutes before adding the steak and putting them on the grill.

1/3 cup sugar

1/3 cup lower-sodium soy sauce

1 1/2 tablespoons sambal oelek (ground fresh chile paste)

1 tablespoon fresh lime juice

1 tablespoon dark sesame oil

6 garlic cloves, minced

1 (1-pound) beef flap steak or sirloin tip steak, sliced against the grain into thin strips

1/4 teaspoon salt

Cooking spray

8 (6-inch) corn tortillas

Quick-Pickled Cabbage

2 green onions, thinly diagonally sliced

Sesame Rice (page 203)

1. Combine the first 6 ingredients in a shallow dish; add the steak. Cover and marinate in the refrigerator for 1 hour, turning the steak after 30 minutes.

2. Preheat the grill to medium-high heat.

3. Remove the steak from the marinade; discard the marinade. Thread the steak onto 8 (8-inch) skewers; sprinkle with the salt. Place the skewers on a grill rack coated with cooking spray. Grill 2 minutes on each side or until the desired degree of doneness. Grill tortillas for 30 seconds on each side or until lightly charred. Assemble tacos with beef and cabbage; sprinkle with green onions. Serve with Sesame Rice.

SERVE WITH

Quick-Pickled Cabbage

Place 3 cups sliced green cabbage in a medium bowl with 2 crushed garlic cloves. Bring 1/2 cup unseasoned rice vinegar, 2 tablespoons lower-sodium soy sauce, 1 tablespoon sugar, and 1 teaspoon sambal oelek (ground fresh chile paste) to a boil. Pour the hot vinegar mixture over the cabbage; toss and cover. Let stand 30 minutes; drain. Serve or chill.

TIGHTWAD TIP
Shop Smart

Aldi has a great selection of inexpensive cuts of beef that work well in this recipe. You can use flat iron, hanger, sirloin tip, or flap steaks. Of course flank steak works well, but it's become more popular, so the price has started to climb. If you don't have access to an Aldi, shop for your meat at supercenter stores like Walmart or discount warehouses like Costco.

Garlicky Beef & Bean Stir-Fry

Total cost $8.92

HANDS-ON 20 MIN.   **TOTAL** 35 MIN.   **SERVES** 4

Cut costs at the supermarket by rethinking how you use meats. Here, I call for a less-expensive cut of beef, and it's used in more of a supporting role in the dish. Next, add plenty of colorful fresh veggies to bulk up the portion size. Thinly slice the meat and stir-fry it quickly, and it'll stay super tender.

3 tablespoons sugar

6 tablespoons soy sauce

3 tablespoons fresh lime juice

1 teaspoon crushed red pepper

8 teaspoons minced fresh garlic

4 tablespoons canola oil, divided

1 (10-ounce) skirt steak, thinly sliced
   across the grain

2 pounds fresh green beans

1 red bell pepper, cut into thin strips

2 teaspoons cornstarch

2 cups hot cooked rice

1. Combine the first 5 ingredients in a small bowl. Gradually whisk in 3 tablespoons oil; transfer to a large zip-top plastic bag. Add the steak; seal. Let stand at room temperature for 15 minutes. Remove the steak, and reserve the marinade in a bowl.

2. Heat a wok or a stainless-steel sauté pan over high heat. Add the remaining 1 tablespoon oil to the wok; swirl to coat. Reduce the heat to medium-high. Add the steak to the hot wok; stir-fry the steak for 1½ minutes or until browned. Remove the steak. Add the beans and bell pepper to the wok; stir-fry for 3 minutes.

3. Whisk the cornstarch into the reserved marinade. Stir the cornstarch mixture into the vegetable mixture. Stir-fry 30 seconds or until the sauce thickens. Stir the steak into the vegetable mixture, and stir-fry 30 seconds or until the steak is cooked to desired degree of doneness. Remove from the heat, and serve over the rice.

TIGHTWAD TIP
Green Beans

If you can't find fresh green beans (or if they're out of season), look for fresh-frozen.

Meaty Eggplant "Lasagna"

Total cost $10

HANDS-ON **30 MIN.**   TOTAL **55 MIN.**   SERVES **4**

This delightful summer casserole has all the elements of a delicious crowd-pleasing lasagna with none of the carbs since grilled eggplant slices stand in for starchy noodles. You can slice zucchini lengthwise into long, thin planks and substitute them for the eggplant if you prefer. Pair this with a small 8-ounce baguette and Summer Salad on page 195.

1 (1-pound) eggplant, trimmed

Cooking spray

3 tablespoons extra-virgin olive oil

3/4 cup chopped onion (about 3 ounces)

1/3 cup diced peeled carrot (about 2 ounces)

2 teaspoons minced fresh garlic (about 2 cloves)

8 ounces 80% lean ground beef

1 1/4 teaspoons kosher salt

1/2 teaspoon black pepper

Pinch of crushed red pepper

2 1/2 cups All-Purpose Tomato Sauce (page 221) or store-bought, divided

6 tablespoons chopped fresh basil leaves, divided

1 cup freshly grated Parmesan cheese (about 4 ounces)

4 ounces fresh mozzarella, thinly sliced

1. Preheat the grill to medium-high heat. Preheat the oven to 450°F.

2. Slice the eggplant crosswise into 12 even slices (about 3/4 inch thick). Lightly coat with cooking spray. Grill the eggplant for 2 to 3 minutes on each side or until tender and well marked.

3. Heat a large sauté pan over medium-high heat. Add the oil; swirl to coat. Sauté the onion and carrot for 3 minutes, stirring often. Add the garlic; sauté 30 seconds, stirring constantly. Add the beef, salt, black pepper, and crushed red pepper; sauté 4 minutes or until the beef is browned, stirring to crumble. Add 2 cups of tomato sauce, and bring to a boil. Cook 1 minute or until warmed through, stirring frequently. Remove from the heat. Adjust the salt and pepper as needed. Stir in 1/4 cup basil.

4. Spread the remaining 1/2 cup tomato sauce over the bottom of a 13- x 9-inch or an 8-inch square baking dish. Arrange 4 eggplant slices in a single layer over the sauce; top with 1/2 cup Parmesan cheese and 1 cup meat sauce. Repeat the layers once, ending with sauce. Arrange the last 4 eggplant slices over the top; spoon the remaining meat sauce over the eggplant. Arrange the sliced mozzarella on top. Bake at 450°F for 15 to 20 minutes or until browned and bubbly. Let stand 5 minutes. Sprinkle with the remaining 2 tablespoons basil before serving.

Total cost $8.18

HOW LOW CAN YOU GO?!

Baked Italian-Style Cauliflower

HANDS-ON **20 MIN.**   TOTAL **24 MIN.**   SERVES **4**

Cauliflower is so versatile: You can steam or boil it, sauté or roast it. It's a terrific stand-in for starchy potatoes in so many tasty and healthy guises. It can be a side. Or the star. Here, I use steamed cauliflower as the base for this delicious main dish. You can cook the cauliflower, make the sauce, and assemble the dish ahead. Then cover and chill until you're ready to heat and serve. Just remember, if you do make it ahead, you'll need to bake the casserole until it's heated through before you broil to finish. Of course, you can make the breadcrumbs ahead too, but don't sprinkle them over the top until you're ready to broil. Serve with Romaine Salad.

1 tablespoon olive oil

1 cup chopped onion

4 garlic cloves, minced

8 ounces 80% lean ground beef

1/2 teaspoon kosher salt

1/4 teaspoon crushed red pepper

1/4 teaspoon freshly ground black pepper

11/2 cups All-Purpose Tomato Sauce (page 221) or store-bought marinara sauce

1/2 cup pitted kalamata olives, coarsely chopped

11/2 pounds cauliflower, cut into florets

Cooking spray

1/2 cup Parsley & Parmesan Breadcrumbs (page 225)

1. Heat a large skillet over medium-high heat. Add the oil to the pan; swirl to coat. Add the onion; sauté 4 minutes. Add the garlic; sauté 30 seconds, stirring constantly. Stir in the beef. Sprinkle with the salt and peppers, and sauté 4 minutes or until browned, stirring to crumble. Stir in the sauce and olives.

2. Arrange the top rack of the oven 5 inches from the broiler element. Preheat the broiler to high.

3. Steam the cauliflower for 4 minutes or until crisp-tender. Place the cauliflower in an 11- x 7-inch broiler-safe baking dish coated with cooking spray; top with the sauce mixture.

4. Sprinkle the breadcrumbs over the sauce mixture. Broil for 4 minutes or until browned.

SERVE WITH

Romaine Salad

Toss 5 cups torn romaine with 2 tablespoons extra-virgin olive oil and 2 teaspoons red wine vinegar; season to taste with salt and pepper. Shave 1 ounce Parmesan cheese over the top.

Cheater's Porchetta

HANDS-ON **25 MIN.**   TOTAL **1 HR., 10 MIN.**   SERVES **4**

Total cost
$9.40

An Italian dish that usually takes hours (or days) to prepare, Old-World style porchetta involves marinating an entire pork loin, encasing it with pork belly or skin, and slowly roasting it for hours. Here, I use a quick-cooking pork tenderloin and wrap it with bacon to offer a similar textural contrast. Minneolas are tangelos, and they taste like tangerines. They're available from January through the spring. When their season passes, look for clementines, tangerines, satsumas, or oranges—whatever is in season and cheapest. Serve with Sicilian-Style Roasted Broccoli (page 196) and Parmesan-Pepper Polenta (page 203).

1 (1-pound) pork tenderloin, trimmed

1 teaspoon kosher salt

¼ teaspoon freshly ground black pepper

1 Minneola or other mandarin orange

2 tablespoons canola oil, divided

2 tablespoons minced fresh shallot

1½ tablespoons minced fresh garlic

1½ tablespoons chopped fresh sage

3 thick-cut slices applewood-smoked bacon

½ cup dry white wine (such as chardonnay)

¾ cup Overnight Chicken Stock (page 218) or store-bought

2 tablespoons butter

1. Preheat the oven to 400°F.

2. Slice the pork lengthwise, cutting to but not through the opposite side. Open the pork up like a book; lay a piece of plastic wrap over the pork. Pound the pork to a ½-inch thickness using a meat mallet. Discard the plastic. Season the pork evenly with salt and pepper.

3. Using a zester, remove the zest from the Minneola (do not remove the bitter white pith); place in a small bowl. Squeeze the juice from the Minneola into a separate bowl; set aside. Heat a small skillet over medium-high heat. Add 1 tablespoon oil to pan; swirl to coat. Sauté shallot for 30 seconds. Add garlic; sauté 30 seconds, stirring constantly. Add shallot mixture, sage, and a pinch of salt to the zest. Rub the sage mixture over the inside of the pork; roll the pork up to form a long cylinder.

4. Wrap the tenderloin in the bacon; secure with butcher's twine. Heat an oven-safe skillet over medium heat. Add the remaining 1 tablespoon canola oil to the pan; swirl to coat. Add the pork; cook 10 minutes, turning to brown on all sides. Place the pan in the preheated oven; bake at 400°F for about 15 minutes or until the bacon is crisp and a meat thermometer registers 155°F. Remove the pork from the pan; let stand, uncovered, for 10 minutes. Reserve the juices in the pan. Slice the pork crosswise into ½-inch-thick slices.

5. Add the wine to the juices in the pan; cook 1 to 2 minutes over medium-high heat or until the wine almost evaporates, scraping the pan to release the browned bits. Stir in the stock and reserved Minneola juice; cook until reduced to ½ cup, whisking occasionally. Remove the pan from the heat. Add the butter to the pan; whisk until the sauce is smooth. Season to taste with salt and pepper. Serve the sauce with the pork.

Pork Tenderloin Agrodolce

Total cost $9.27

HANDS-ON **20 MIN.** TOTAL **1 HR.** SERVES **4**

Agrodolce, Italian for sweet and sour, is a wonderful sauce made from cooking balsamic vinegar with a little sugar until it's syrupy. I add a little chicken stock, dried fruit, and tangy olives—Castelvetrano are my favorites—to the mix for a nuanced flavor. Round out your plate with Walnut-Thyme Roasted Broccoli (page 196) and Parmesan Risotto.

$1/2$ cup balsamic vinegar

$1/3$ cup green olives

$1/4$ cup dried sweet cherries

$1/4$ cup Overnight Chicken Stock (page 218) or store-bought

$1^{1}/2$ tablespoons sugar

4 garlic cloves

2 fresh thyme sprigs

8 ounces fresh or frozen pearl onions, thawed and peeled

1 teaspoon kosher salt, divided

2 tablespoons olive oil

1 ($1^{1}/4$-pound) pork tenderloin, trimmed

$1/2$ teaspoon freshly ground black pepper

1. Preheat the oven to 500°F.

2. Combine the first 8 ingredients in a small saucepan; stir in $1/4$ teaspoon salt. Bring to a boil. Cover, reduce the heat to medium-low, and cook for 15 to 20 minutes or until the onions are just tender, stirring occasionally. Uncover, increase the heat to medium-high, and cook until the sauce is syrupy and thick, stirring frequently.

3. Heat the oil in a large cast-iron skillet over medium-high heat. Sprinkle the pork with the remaining $3/4$ teaspoon salt and pepper. Add the pork to the pan; cook 1 minute. Turn the pork over. Place the pan in the oven; bake at 500°F for 10 to 12 minutes or until a thermometer registers 150° (slightly pink). Remove from oven; let stand 10 minutes. Slice pork crosswise into $1/2$-inch-thick slices. Serve with the sauce.

SERVE WITH
Parmesan Risotto

Bring 3 cups Overnight Chicken Stock to a simmer in a small saucepan; leave over low heat. Heat a saucepan over medium. Add 1 tablespoon olive oil; swirl. Add 1 cup chopped onion; cook 6 minutes, stirring occasionally. Stir in 1 cup Arborio rice and 1 teaspoon minced fresh garlic. Increase heat to medium-high; sauté 1 minute. Stir $1/2$ cup warm stock into the pan with the rice; cook until liquid almost evaporates, stirring frequently. Repeat procedure with remaining stock, adding the liquid, $1/2$ cup at a time, until rice is al dente. Remove the pan from heat; stir in $1/4$ cup grated Parmesan cheese. Season to taste with salt and pepper.

Pork Tenderloin with Mushroom Sauce

Total cost $8.91

HANDS-ON **18 MIN.**   TOTAL **48 MIN.**   SERVES **4**

Here's another recipe that's simple enough to be a weeknight staple, but it's also company worthy. It tastes and looks more like a restaurant meal. Serve with Parmesan-Pepper Polenta (page 203) or grits. Crème fraîche is similar to sour cream, with a creamier, less tangy flavor. It's available in some supermarkets and at specialty grocers, like Whole Foods, but it can be expensive. If you want to save time and money, you can easily make your own. See below for my DIY Crème Fraîche.

1 (1-pound) pork tenderloin, trimmed

1¼ teaspoons kosher salt, divided

½ teaspoon black pepper

2 tablespoons olive oil, divided

1 (8-ounce) package button mushrooms, thinly sliced

3 garlic cloves, minced

2 tablespoons white wine vinegar

1 cup Overnight Chicken Stock (page 218) or store-bought

¼ cup crème fraîche or sour cream

2 teaspoons Dijon mustard

1½ tablespoons chopped fresh flat-leaf parsley

DIY Crème Fraîche

Place 1 cup heavy whipping cream in a small jar with a tight-fitting lid; stir in 1 tablespoon buttermilk. Cover and let stand at room temperature for 12 hours or until the desired consistency is reached. You'll know it's ready when the cream is no longer liquid and it has a yogurt-like consistency. Cover and keep refrigerated for up to 2 weeks.

1. Place a small roasting pan in the oven. Preheat the oven to 425°F.

2. Sprinkle the pork evenly with 1 teaspoon salt and the pepper. Add 1 tablespoon olive oil to the preheated pan, and swirl to coat. Add the pork to pan. Roast at 425°F for 20 minutes or until a thermometer inserted in the thickest portion of pork registers 145°F (for medium) or to the desired degree of doneness, turning after 10 minutes. Remove the pork from the pan, and let stand 10 minutes.

3. Meanwhile, place the roasting pan over medium-high heat. Add the remaining 1 tablespoon oil to the pan; swirl to coat. Add the mushrooms; sauté 4 minutes, stirring occasionally. Add the garlic, and sauté 1 minute, stirring constantly. Stir in the vinegar, and bring to a boil, scraping the pan to release the browned bits. Cook 1 minute or until the liquid almost evaporates, stirring occasionally. Stir in the remaining ¼ teaspoon salt and the stock; bring to a boil. Cook until the liquid is reduced to ⅓ cup, about 7 minutes. Remove from the heat, and stir in the crème fraîche and mustard. Slice the pork, and serve with the sauce. Sprinkle with the parsley.

Honey-Glazed Pork Tenderloin

Total cost $9.91

HANDS-ON **45 MIN.**   TOTAL **1 HR., 20 MIN.**   SERVES **4**

I used to make homemade applesauce with my grandmother, Nanny, when I was just a wee little girl. It was my favorite thing we made together, besides Nanny's 7Up Pound Cake, of course. This is a jazzier version of homemade applesauce that pairs perfectly with pork tenderloin, especially this one with a delicious spice rub and honey glaze. It takes a while to cook the apples, so when pressed for time, make whipped sweet potatoes instead. Prep your sides first, starting with the applesauce. Once it's simmering, start on Roasted Brussels Sprouts (page 195), and cook the pork last.

1 (1¼-pound) pork tenderloin, trimmed

1½ tablespoons olive oil

1¼ teaspoons ground cumin

1 teaspoon kosher salt

½ teaspoon freshly ground black pepper

½ teaspoon apple pie spice

2 tablespoons honey

1 tablespoon butter, melted

TIGHTWAD TIP
Buying Apples

Avoid Honeycrisp apples because they usually cost at least a dollar more per pound than other apples with a similar appearance, flavor, and texture. McIntosh apples are great if you want a silky smooth applesauce. I like mine chunky, so I use Pink Lady or Granny Smith.

1. Preheat the oven to 425°F.

2. Brush all sides of the pork with the oil. Stir together the cumin, salt, pepper, and apple pie spice; rub over the pork. Place the pork in a roasting pan. Bake at 425°F for 12 minutes. Whisk together the honey and melted butter; brush half of the mixture over the pork, and bake for 1 minute. Turn the pork, and brush with the remaining honey mixture. Bake for 2 more minutes or until a meat thermometer inserted in thickest portion registers 150°F or to desired degree of doneness. Let stand 5 minutes; slice.

SERVE WITH
Chunky Homemade Applesauce

Peel, core, and chop 1½ pounds apples. Sauté the apples in 3 tablespoons melted butter in a large saucepan over medium-high heat for 5 minutes. Stir in zest and juice from 1 lemon, 1 tablespoon sugar, ¼ teaspoon salt, and 1 cup water; bring to a boil. Reduce the heat to medium-low, and simmer, stirring occasionally, 40 minutes or until the apples are tender. Remove from the heat; mash the apples to the desired consistency.

Pork Scaloppine

Total cost
$8.14

HANDS-ON **30 MIN.**   TOTAL **30 MIN.**   SERVES **4**

Wow your guests with this impressive dish that's really simple to prepare. Potato Smashers (page 200) are glorious with this moist, flavorful pork. Round out the meal with basic Roasted Broccoli (page 196).

1 (1-pound) boneless pork loin, cut into 12 slices

$2^1/_2$ teaspoons kosher salt, divided

2 teaspoons freshly ground black pepper, divided

$^3/_4$ cup panko breadcrumbs

$^2/_3$ cup all-purpose flour

2 tablespoons grated Parmesan cheese

2 teaspoons garlic powder

$^1/_2$ cup buttermilk

1 large egg

6 tablespoons canola oil

$^1/_2$ cup dry white wine (such as chardonnay)

3 fresh thyme sprigs

1 cup Overnight Chicken Stock (page 218) or store-bought

$^1/_4$ cup butter, at room temperature

1 tablespoon finely chopped fresh flat-leaf parsley

1. Place the pork slices between 2 sheets of plastic wrap, and pound to $^1/_4$-inch thickness. Sprinkle the pork with $^1/_2$ teaspoon each salt and pepper.

2. Place the panko, flour, and Parmesan in a shallow dish. Stir in $1^1/_2$ teaspoons salt, 1 teaspoon pepper, and garlic powder. Stir together the buttermilk and egg in another shallow dish. Dip the pork in the buttermilk mixture, shaking off excess moisture; dredge in the flour mixture.

3. Heat a large sauté pan over medium-high heat. Add 1 tablespoon oil to the pan; swirl to coat. Add 2 coated pork cutlets at a time to the hot pan; cook for 1 to 2 minutes per side or just until the pork is golden and cooked to the desired degree of doneness. Repeat the process with the remaining oil and coated cutlets. Place the cooked pork on a platter, and cover with foil to keep warm.

4. Remove the pan from the heat, and add the wine and thyme sprigs to the pan. Return the pan to the heat, and bring to a boil. Cook about 1 minute or until the wine almost evaporates, scraping the bottom of the pan to release the browned bits. Add the stock to the pan; bring to a boil. Cook until the liquid reduces to $^1/_4$ cup, about 4 minutes. Remove from the heat. Discard the thyme, and whisk in the butter. Season with the remaining $^1/_2$ teaspoon each salt and pepper. Garnish with the chopped fresh parsley, and serve with the pork.

Roast Pork with Rice Noodles

Total cost $8.99

HANDS-ON **30 MIN.**   TOTAL **9 HR., 40 MIN.**   SERVES **4**

Chinese-style barbecue, *char siu*, is robust with sweet, salty, and spicy flavors working in concert, and the mildly seasoned rice noodles provide a cooling contrast. Although most—if not all—of the ingredients are available in many groceries and at big-box stores, you definitely want to make a trip to the Asian market to shop for this dish because that's where you'll find the best-quality, tastiest ingredients, and they'll be less expensive. Serve with Cucumber Salad on page 195.

8 garlic cloves, divided

1/2 cup low-sodium soy sauce, divided

3 tablespoons dark sesame oil, divided

1 tablespoon sambal oelek (ground fresh chile paste), divided

1/4 cup honey

3 tablespoons rice vinegar

2 tablespoons hoisin sauce

1 (1 1/4-pound) boneless pork shoulder (Boston butt)

1 1/2 tablespoons cornstarch

1/3 cup fresh lime juice, divided

8 ounces uncooked rice noodles

2 tablespoons brown sugar

2 tablespoons torn fresh mint leaves

2 green onions, thinly sliced

1. Smash and mince 6 garlic cloves into a smooth paste. Combine the garlic paste, 1/4 cup soy sauce, 1 tablespoon oil, 2 teaspoons chile paste, honey, rice vinegar, and hoisin, stirring well with a whisk; place the mixture in a ziplock plastic bag. Place the pork in the bag; seal. Marinate in the refrigerator for 8 hours or overnight, turning occasionally.

2. Preheat the oven to 450°F.

3. Remove the pork from the bag; reserve the marinade. Place a roasting rack in a roasting pan. Fill the pan with water to a depth of 1/2 inch; place the pork on the rack. Roast the pork at 450°F for 15 minutes. Baste the pork with some of the reserved marinade. Turn the pork over; baste.

4. Reduce the oven temperature to 400°F. Roast the pork for 40 more minutes, basting every 10 minutes. Reserve the remaining marinade. Remove the pork from the pan, reserving the cooking liquid in the pan. Let the pork stand for 15 minutes; slice.

5. Place the roasting pan over medium-high heat; bring the cooking liquid to a boil. Stir the remaining marinade into the liquid; boil 2 minutes. Whisk together the cornstarch and 1 1/2 tablespoons juice. Stir the cornstarch mixture into the cooking liquid; boil for 1 minute, whisking constantly. Adjust the seasoning as needed. Remove from the heat; cool slightly. Toss the pork with the sauce.

6. Meanwhile, prepare the noodles according to the package directions; drain. Mince the remaining 2 garlic cloves. Combine the garlic, remaining 1/4 cup soy sauce, 2 tablespoons oil, 1 teaspoon chile paste, 1/4 cup juice, and sugar in a large bowl, stirring well. Add the noodles to the bowl; toss to coat. Adjust the seasoning as needed. Serve the pork over noodles; sprinkle with the mint and onions.

Pork & Sweet Potatoes

Total cost $9.60

HANDS-ON **50 MIN.**   TOTAL **1 HR., 55 MIN.**   SERVES **4**

Sweet potatoes and earthy porcini mushrooms make for a deliciously comforting combo that's also hearty enough to warm you to the core during winter's coldest days. Although the pork takes awhile to cook, the simmering is hands off, so you won't be stuck at the stove all day. Buy an 8-ounce loaf of crusty bread to serve with (that's included in the cost of the meal), and whip up a quick salad (not included), if you like.

1 (1-pound) boneless pork shoulder (Boston butt), cut into $\frac{1}{2}$-inch cubes

1 teaspoon kosher salt

$\frac{1}{2}$ teaspoon black pepper

$2\frac{1}{2}$ tablespoons olive oil, divided

2 tablespoons tomato paste

$\frac{1}{4}$ cup cider vinegar

$\frac{1}{2}$ (1-ounce) package dried porcini mushrooms

$3\frac{1}{2}$ cups Overnight Chicken Stock (page 218) or store-bought, divided

6 garlic cloves, crushed

3 tablespoons butter

4 cups ($\frac{1}{2}$-inch) cubed peeled sweet potato (about 1 pound)

1 cup chopped yellow onion

$\frac{1}{4}$ teaspoon ground cayenne pepper

2 green onions, thinly diagonally sliced

1 (8-ounce) loaf French bread

1. Heat a 12-inch cast-iron pot with tight-fitting lid over medium-high heat. Sprinkle the pork evenly with 1 teaspoon salt and the black pepper. Add $1\frac{1}{2}$ tablespoons oil to the pan; swirl to coat. Add the pork; sauté for about 8 minutes, turning to brown on all sides. Add the tomato paste to the pan, rubbing around to bring as much tomato paste in direct contact with the bottom of the pan as possible; cook for 30 seconds to 1 minute. Stir in the vinegar; cook until the liquid almost evaporates.

2. Place the dried porcini mushrooms in a small bowl. Bring 1 cup stock to a boil, and pour into the bowl. Cover and let stand for about 5 minutes or until the mushrooms are rehydrated. Add the remaining $2\frac{1}{2}$ cups stock, garlic, mushrooms, and soaking liquid to the pan; bring to a boil. Cover, reduce heat to low, and simmer for 50 minutes to 1 hour or until the pork is fork-tender.

3. Heat a large skillet over medium-high heat. Add the remaining 1 tablespoon olive oil and the butter to pan. Cook until the butter melts, swirling to coat. Add the potato, onion, and cayenne; sauté 6 minutes or until lightly browned, stirring occasionally. Add the potato mixture to the pot with the pork; bring to a boil. Reduce the heat to medium, and cook, uncovered, for 15 to 20 minutes or until the liquid nearly evaporates, stirring occasionally. Sprinkle with the green onions. Serve with French bread.

Pork Chops with Cherry Couscous

Total cost $9.96

HANDS-ON **19 MIN.**   TOTAL **32 MIN.**   SERVES **4**

Cherries work well for this dish in the summer, but fresh peaches or blackberries would too. In the fall, use pears, and oranges or tangerines in the winter. Serve with Grilled Corn with Honey-Lime Butter.

4 bone-in center cut pork chops

1¹/₂ teaspoons salt, divided

¹/₄ teaspoon freshly ground black pepper

Cooking spray

1 cup uncooked couscous

2 tablespoons olive oil

1 cup coarsely chopped pitted cherries

¹/₂ cup sliced green onions

¹/₃ cup dry-roasted almonds, chopped

2 teaspoons grated fresh lemon zest

2 tablespoons fresh lemon juice

1. Preheat the grill to medium-high heat.

2. Sprinkle both sides of the pork evenly with 1 teaspoon salt and black pepper. Place the pork on a grill rack coated with cooking spray, and grill 4 minutes on each side or until desired degree of doneness. Let the pork stand for 5 minutes.

3. Place the couscous in a large bowl. Add ³/₄ cup boiling water; cover and let stand for 5 minutes. Uncover and fluff with a fork. Stir in the remaining ¹/₂ teaspoon salt and the oil. Add the cherries and remaining ingredients; toss to combine. Serve with the pork.

SERVE WITH
Grilled Corn with Honey-Lime Butter

Grill 4 ears shucked corn over medium-high heat for 2 to 3 minutes or just until lightly charred, turning to cook all sides. Whisk together 2 tablespoons melted butter, 1 teaspoon honey, ¹/₂ teaspoon grated fresh lime zest, and a pinch of salt. Brush the butter mixture over the corn.

Cheesy Bacon & Two-Onion Tart

Total cost $9.97

HANDS-ON **50 MIN.**   TOTAL **1 HR., 40 MIN.**   SERVES **4**

Elevate an ordinary quiche by using store-bought puff pastry for the crust. Whip up a quick Pea Soup (page 202) to serve on the side.

5 (1-ounce) slices smoked bacon

1 red onion, sliced

¾ cup heavy cream

¼ teaspoon kosher salt

¼ teaspoon freshly ground black pepper

3 large eggs, lightly beaten

½ (17.3-ounce) package frozen puff pastry sheets, thawed

1½ cups (6 ounces) freshly shredded Swiss cheese, divided

1 cup sliced spring onions (about 3) or 1 bunch large green onions

⅓ cup grated Parmesan cheese

1 large egg yolk

2 tablespoons milk

1. Arrange the top rack of the oven 7 inches from the broiler element. Preheat the broiler to high.

2. Cook the bacon in a skillet over medium heat until crisp; crumble. Set aside 2 tablespoons bacon drippings; reserve remaining drippings for another use.

3. Place the red onion on a foil-lined baking sheet; brush with the reserved 2 tablespoons drippings. Broil 4 minutes per side or until the onion is blistered and crisp-tender.

4. Reduce the oven temperature to 400°F.

5. Whisk together the cream, salt, pepper, and 3 whole eggs. Unfold the pastry; roll to a 12-inch square on a floured surface, and fit into a greased 9-inch tart or quiche pan. Sprinkle 1 cup Swiss cheese and half of the crumbled bacon onto the crust; top with the spring onions and red onion. Pour the cream mixture over the onions. Fold the excess dough toward the center. Sprinkle the center with the Parmesan cheese, remaining bacon, and remaining Swiss cheese. Combine the yolk and milk; brush over the dough. Bake at 400°F for 40 minutes or until golden. Let stand 10 minutes.

TIGHTWAD TIP
Save the Bacon Drippings

Never toss out leftover bacon drippings. Refrigerate them in a jar a with tight-fitting lid so they're ready and waiting when you need a little or a lot to cook with.

Garlicky Spinach & Sausage Gratin

Total cost $10.00

HANDS-ON **25 MIN.**   TOTAL **37 MIN.**   SERVES **4**

Your family and friends will love you for making this comforting casserole. And you'll love how easy it is to prepare. Just take care with the sauce after adding the milk and egg mixture to the pan. The eggs are there to add richness and a gorgeous supple texture to the dish, but if the pan gets too hot, the eggs may scramble instead of thickening the sauce. Serve with half a recipe of Grissini on page 226 and Easy Smashed Potatoes.

2 tablespoons extra-virgin olive oil, divided

1 cup chopped onion

8 garlic cloves, coarsely chopped

12 ounces pork breakfast sausage

1 teaspoon kosher salt

1/4 teaspoon ground red pepper

2 tablespoons all-purpose flour

2 cups whole milk

2 large eggs, lightly beaten

1 cup Overnight Chicken Stock (page 218) or store-bought

9 ounces fresh baby spinach, trimmed

Cooking spray

3/4 cup Parsley & Parmesan Breadcrumbs (page 225) or panko

1. Preheat the oven to 450°F.

2. Heat a Dutch oven over medium-high heat. Add 1 tablespoon oil to the pan; swirl to coat. Add the onion; sauté 4 minutes. Add the garlic; sauté 30 seconds, stirring constantly. Add the sausage, salt, and pepper; sauté 5 minutes, stirring to crumble.

3. Stir in the flour; sauté 30 seconds, stirring constantly. Combine the milk and eggs, stirring well. Reduce the heat to medium. Stir the milk mixture and stock into the sausage mixture; bring to a boil, and cook 2 minutes, stirring constantly. Remove from the heat; stir in the spinach. Spoon the spinach mixture into an 11- x 7-inch baking dish coated with cooking spray. Top with the breadcrumbs. Bake at 450°F for 12 minutes or until bubbly.

SERVE WITH
Easy Smashed Potatoes

Peel and chop 1 pound Yukon Gold potatoes. Put the potatoes in a medium saucepan; cover with 1 cup whole milk, and add water to pan to a depth of 2 inches above the potatoes. Bring to a boil over medium-high heat; boil 8 to 10 minutes or until the potatoes are tender. Drain. Return the potatoes to pan with 1 cup heavy cream and 3 tablespoons butter. Heat over low heat, mashing the potatoes to the desired consistency. Remove from the heat; stir in 1/4 cup sour cream. Season to taste with salt and pepper. Serve immediately.

 TIGHTWAD TIP
Buying Spinach

Look for store-brand bags of regular baby spinach. National brands, especially organic, are much more expensive.

Roast Leg of Lamb

Total cost
$9.86

HANDS-ON **12 MIN.**   TOTAL **45 MIN.**   SERVES **4**

It's impossible to have a simpler recipe: Lamb, salt, pepper, oil. Boom. Awesome. Make the mind-blowingly delicious harissa by hand in a mortar and pestle in a few minutes, or just whip it together in your mini chopper. Either way, you'll have dinner on the table in a flash with almost no effort. Just sit back and get ready for the accolades. You can tie the lamb with kitchen twine, if you like, which helps it retain its shape better. Round out the meal with Browned Butter Rice Pilaf (page 203) and Roasted Green Beans (page 53).

1 (1-pound) boneless leg of lamb, trimmed

1 teaspoon salt

$1/2$ teaspoon freshly ground black pepper

1 tablespoon canola oil

Homemade Harissa

1. Preheat the oven to 450°F.

2. Sprinkle all sides of the lamb evenly with 1 teaspoon salt and the pepper. Heat an oven-safe sauté pan over medium-high heat. Add the oil to the pan; swirl to coat. Add the lamb; cook 4 minutes, turning to brown on all sides. Place the pan in the preheated oven, and bake at 450°F for 20 to 25 minutes or until a meat thermometer inserted in thickest part of the roast registers 120°F for rare, or cook to the desired degree of doneness. Place the lamb on a cutting board. Let stand at room temperature 10 minutes; slice. Serve with Homemade Harissa.

Homemade Harissa

Combine 1 tablespoon sambal oelek (ground fresh chile paste), 1 tablespoon minced fresh garlic paste, $1/4$ teaspoon kosher salt, $1/4$ teaspoon ground cumin, and $1/8$ teaspoon ground coriander, stirring well. Slowly drizzle 2 tablespoons extra-virgin olive oil into the bowl, whisking constantly until mixture is well blended. Makes about $1/4$ cup

Lamb Tagine

Total cost $7.85

HANDS-ON **25 MIN.**   TOTAL **1 HR., 25 MIN.**   SERVES **4**

In Morocco, *tagine* refers both to the recipe and the cone-shaped clay pot the stew cooks in. Since tradition calls to serve the tagine over couscous, cook it just before you're ready to serve. Since you have extra room in the budget, pick up some flatbread, if you want (it's not included in the total cost listed above).

1 tablespoon olive oil

8 ounces cubed lamb stew meat

1¼ teaspoons kosher salt, divided

2 cups chopped onion

1 teaspoon ground cumin

½ teaspoon ground cinnamon

½ teaspoon ground cayenne pepper

8 garlic cloves, coarsely chopped

2 tablespoons honey

2 tablespoons tomato paste

2 cups cubed peeled butternut squash

½ cup raisins

2 cups Overnight Chicken Stock (page 218) or store-bought

⅓ cup coarsely chopped pitted green olives

1 cup uncooked couscous

¼ cup toasted sliced almonds

1 tablespoon chopped fresh flat-leaf parsley

1. Heat a Dutch oven over medium-high heat. Add the oil to the pan; swirl to coat. Sprinkle the lamb evenly with ¾ teaspoon salt. Add the lamb to the pan; sauté 4 minutes, turning to brown on all sides. Remove from the pan. Add the onion; cook for 4 minutes, stirring frequently. Add the remaining ½ teaspoon salt, cumin, cinnamon, cayenne, and garlic; cook for 1 minute, stirring constantly. Stir in the honey and tomato paste; cook 30 seconds, stirring frequently.

2. Return the lamb to the pan. Add the squash, raisins, and stock; bring to a boil. Cover, reduce the heat to medium, and simmer for 1 hour or until the lamb is tender, stirring occasionally. Remove from the heat; stir in the olives.

3. Meanwhile, cook the couscous according to the package directions. Serve the tagine over the couscous; top each serving with almonds and parsley.

FISH & SHELLFISH

Cost-cutting cooks tend to think they need to do without seafood. Not true. Savvy shopping will save you a boatload. While fresh halibut and wild salmon run near $30 a pound, there are plenty of other fish—and shellfish—in the seafood section. Fresh-water options like trout and tilapia are cheaper than beef and available at markets nationwide. Sustainably farmed salmon delivers rich flavor at less than half the cost of wild-caught. And even more savings await among the frozen options. Keep a bag of medium-sized frozen shrimp on hand, and you'll always have a scrumptious dinner just minutes away.

Mediterranean-Style Fish Cake Sandwiches

Total cost $10

HANDS-ON **45 MIN.**   TOTAL **45 MIN.**   SERVES **4**

If you like falafel (fried chickpea patties usually sandwiched in a pita pocket), you'll love this healthier baked twist on that theme. The flavor profile of the fish cakes, like falafel, comes from a tasty puree of chickpeas, lemon, and spices. Adding mackerel gives a healthy seaside twist to this fusion sandwich. Serve with Chickpea & Tomato Toss on page 202.

1 1/4 teaspoons kosher salt, divided

1/2 teaspoon ground cumin

1/4 teaspoon ground dried ginger

1/8 teaspoon ground mustard

1/8 teaspoon ground turmeric

1/8 teaspoon ground cayenne pepper

3 tablespoons extra-virgin olive oil, divided

2 (6-ounce) Atlantic mackerel fillets

2 tablespoons mayonnaise

1 teaspoon grated fresh lemon zest

1 (15-ounce) can chickpeas, drained and rinsed

1/3 cup panko breadcrumbs

1 tablespoon fresh lemon juice

2 green onions, trimmed and thinly diagonally sliced, white and green parts separated

1 large egg

2 tablespoons finely chopped cucumber

1/2 teaspoon dried dill

1/2 cup plain whole-milk Greek yogurt

4 (4-inch) squares Feta & Red Onion Focaccia (page 229) or store-bought

4 leaves red leaf lettuce

1. Preheat the oven to 425°F.

2. Combine 1/2 teaspoon salt, cumin, ginger, mustard, turmeric, and cayenne; stir in 1 tablespoon oil. Rub the spice mixture over the fish. Place the fish on a baking sheet; bake at 425°F for 8 to 12 minutes or just until the fish flakes with a fork. Let the fish stand at room temperature for 5 minutes; break into chunks.

3. Place the mayonnaise, zest, and chickpeas in a bowl; mash with a fork or potato masher to form a chunky mixture. Stir in 1 tablespoon oil; continue mashing. Stir in 1/2 teaspoon salt, panko, juice, white parts of the green onions, and egg. Carefully fold in the chunks of fish. Divide the mixture into 4 equal portions; shape each into a cake.

4. Heat the remaining 1 tablespoon oil in a large nonstick skillet over medium-high. Add the cakes; cook 2 to 3 minutes per side or until browned. Transfer to a parchment-lined baking sheet. Bake at 425°F until firm, about 5 minutes.

5. Meanwhile, stir the cucumber, green parts of the green onion, dill, and the remaining 1/4 teaspoon salt into the yogurt. Halve the focaccia horizontally and lengthwise. Spread 1 tablespoon of the yogurt mixture on half of the focaccia; top each with 1 lettuce leaf, 1 fish cake, 1 tablespoon yogurt mixture, and the top half of focaccia.

TIGHTWAD TIP
Mackerel

Mackerel is a full-flavored fish, so you need only a small amount to make the fish cakes. Since it's also sustainable and affordable, it's a great choice for these sandwiches.

Sheet Pan BBQ Fish Tacos with Mexi Corn

Total cost $8.28

HANDS-ON **20 MIN.**   TOTAL **30 MIN.**   SERVES **4**

Serve the tacos with quick, easy, and fantastically delicious corn on the cob that's made in the style of Mexican street corn. Cook the corn and fish together on one sheet pan. While they cook, toss together a fresh slaw to add crunch to the tacos and char the tortillas.

1 teaspoon kosher salt, divided

¼ teaspoon ground cumin

⅛ teaspoon chili powder

¼ teaspoon smoked paprika, divided

⅛ teaspoon ground cayenne pepper, divided

5 teaspoons canola oil, divided

1 teaspoon agave nectar

1 garlic clove, minced

2 (8-ounce) tilapia fillets

Cooking spray

4 ears fresh corn on the cob, shucked

2 tablespoons melted butter

1 teaspoon grated fresh lime zest

2 tablespoons Mexican crema or sour cream

3 green onions, trimmed, thinly sliced, and divided

½ cup chopped avocado

1 tablespoon fresh lime juice

2 cups shredded green cabbage

½ cup quartered cherry tomatoes

8 (6-inch) flour tortillas

1. Arrange the top rack of the oven 7 inches from the broiler element. Preheat the broiler to high.

2. Combine ½ teaspoon salt, cumin, chili powder, ⅛ teaspoon paprika, and a pinch of cayenne in a small bowl; stir in 1 tablespoon canola oil, agave nectar, and minced garlic. Rub the oil mixture over the fish; let stand 15 minutes.

3. Line a baking sheet with foil; coat with cooking spray. Arrange the corn at one end of the prepared pan; brush one side of corn with 1 tablespoon melted butter. Broil 5 to 6 minutes or until blistered. Turn the corn over; brush with the remaining butter.

4. Place the fish on the opposite end of the baking sheet from the corn. Broil 6 minutes or until the fish is done. Combine the zest and crema. Combine the remaining ½ teaspoon salt, remaining ⅛ teaspoon paprika, and remaining pinch of cayenne; sprinkle evenly over the corn. Drizzle the crema on the corn, and top with one of the sliced green onions.

5. Toss the avocado with the lime juice. Place the cabbage, tomatoes, and 2 sliced green onions in a medium mixing bowl. Add the avocado mixture and the remaining 2 teaspoons canola oil to the slaw; toss. Season to taste with salt and pepper.

6. Break the fish into chunks. Assemble the tacos with the tortillas, fish, and slaw. Serve with the corn.

Mexican Crema

Mexican crema is like sour cream, only it has a thinner consistency and less tangy flavor. You can find it in most local groceries, but the lowest price is still at the Hispanic specialty market.

Salmon & Arugula Salad with Bagel Croutons & Dilly Dressing

Total cost $9.71

HANDS-ON **45 MIN.** TOTAL **45 MIN.** SERVES **4**

Here's a main-dish salad that includes all the elements of bagels with lox. Instead of using smoked salmon, you broil fresh salmon; I like crumbled goat cheese over the top to lend a similar tang to cream cheese.

2 (6-ounce) skin-on salmon fillets

2 tablespoons canola oil, divided

$\frac{1}{2}$ teaspoon kosher salt

$\frac{1}{4}$ teaspoon freshly ground black pepper

1 tablespoon unsalted butter, melted

1 to 2 everything bagels, cut into $\frac{1}{2}$-inch cubes

$\frac{1}{4}$ cup whole buttermilk

1 teaspoon fresh lemon juice

1 teaspoon chopped drained capers

$\frac{1}{2}$ teaspoon minced dried dill

1 green onion, finely chopped

Pinch of ground cayenne pepper

4 cups arugula

1 medium plum tomato, chopped

1 cup chopped English cucumber

$\frac{1}{4}$ cup thinly sliced red onion

$\frac{1}{4}$ cup crumbled goat cheese (optional)

1. Arrange the top rack of the oven 7 inches from the broiler element. Preheat the broiler to high.

2. Place the salmon, skin side down, on a broiler-safe baking sheet. Brush 2 teaspoons oil over the fillets; sprinkle with the salt and black pepper. Broil for 6 to 8 minutes or until the desired degree of doneness. Let the fish cool for 5 minutes; flake with a fork.

3. Lower the oven temperature to 400°F.

4. Drizzle the melted butter over the bagel cubes in a large mixing bowl, tossing to coat. Spread the bagel cubes in a single layer over a baking sheet. Bake at 400°F for 10 to 12 minutes or until golden and crisp, stirring after 5 minutes.

5. Whisk the remaining 4 teaspoons oil into the buttermilk. Whisk in the lemon juice, capers, dill, green onion, and cayenne. Place the arugula in a salad bowl; top with the bagel croutons, salmon, tomatoes, cucumber, and red onion. Drizzle with the dressing; toss. Adjust the seasoning as needed. Top with the cheese, if desired. Serve immediately.

TIGHTWAD TIP
Smart Shopping

Look in the fresh or frozen section at Aldi for the best price on salmon fillets. And Walmart's bakery makes everything bagels for a good price.

Lentil & Smoked Trout Waldorf

Total cost $9.65

HANDS-ON **20 MIN.**   TOTAL **50 MIN.**   SERVES **4**

Waldorf salad in a new guise: smoky trout, crisp apple, sweet cherries, and crunchy walnuts. The lentils are tender with a slight chew, just as they should be. Follow the lentil cooking directions to a tee, because you surely don't want them to go mushy. You'll find red split lentils at Trader Joe's for the best price.

$2^{1}/_{2}$ cups red split lentils

3 tablespoons canola oil, divided

1 tablespoon cider vinegar

1 small Red Delicious apple with peel, cored and chopped (6 ounces)

1 tablespoon fresh lemon juice

1 teaspoon sugar

$^{3}/_{4}$ cup diced celery (about 2 ribs)

$^{1}/_{2}$ cup chopped toasted walnuts

$^{1}/_{2}$ cup dried cherries or raisins

$^{1}/_{3}$ cup finely chopped red onion

$^{1}/_{8}$ teaspoon ground cayenne pepper

2 tablespoons extra-virgin olive oil

1 (4-ounce) smoked trout fillet

1 teaspoon kosher salt

$^{1}/_{2}$ teaspoon freshly ground black pepper

1. Place the lentils in a medium saucepan; add 8 cups cold water and 1 tablespoon canola oil to the pan with the lentils. Cook over medium heat for 18 to 20 minutes or just until the lentils turn a light salmon color and are just tender; do not boil. Drain the lentils. Toss the hot lentils gently with the remaining 2 tablespoons canola oil and vinegar; let stand 2 to 3 minutes. Spread the lentils in a single layer on a baking sheet to cool.

2. Place the apple in a large mixing bowl; toss with the lemon juice and sugar. Add the celery and the next 4 ingredients; toss. Add the lentils and drizzle with the olive oil. Flake the trout over the top of the salad; stir gently to combine. Season to taste with salt and pepper. Chill at least 30 minutes before serving.

TIGHTWAD TIP
Trout

With smoked trout, just a small amount adds loads of flavor. Whether smoked or fresh, trout is an affordable freshwater fish that's also abundant, therefore sustainable.

Tuna-Chickpea Salad

Total cost
$9.97

HANDS-ON 10 MIN.   TOTAL 20 MIN.   SERVES 4

The combination of roasted sweet peppers, fresh green beans, chickpeas, and tuna is inspired by Spanish cuisine. Look for roasted piquillo peppers canned or jarred. If you can't find them, substitute bell peppers instead.

2 cups (1-inch) cut fresh green beans (about ½ pound)

2 tablespoons minced shallots

1 teaspoon minced fresh garlic

2 fire-roasted piquillo peppers, chopped

1 (15-ounce) can chickpeas, drained and rinsed

¼ cup mayonnaise

1 tablespoon white wine vinegar

1 teaspoon Spanish smoked paprika

½ teaspoon fresh lemon juice

¼ cup (1 ounce) grated Parmesan cheese

8 (1-ounce) slices French bread

4 cups arugula

2 (5-ounce) cans albacore tuna, packed in olive oil, flaked

1. Arrange the top rack of the oven 5 inches from the broiler element. Preheat the broiler to high.

2. Cook the green beans in boiling salted water for 4 minutes or until crisp-tender. Drain and rinse with cold water; drain. Combine the green beans, shallots, and the next 3 ingredients in a large bowl. Whisk together the mayonnaise and the next 3 ingredients. Add to the bowl with the beans; toss. Season to taste with salt and pepper.

3. Sprinkle the cheese evenly over the bread slices; place the bread on a baking sheet. Broil for 2 minutes or until lightly toasted.

4. Arrange 1 cup arugula on each of 4 plates; divide the bean mixture evenly among the plates. Top each serving with flaked tuna; season to taste with salt and pepper. Serve the toasts with the salad.

Spanish Accent

It's second nature to combine familiar ingredients, like tuna, green beans, and arugula. Add Spanish flavor with a few easy-to-find but less familiar ingredients, and you'll be transported to Spain:

- Piquillo peppers: Brilliant red little peppers with a bold tangy-sweet flavor that turn up on tapas plates in their homeland. Although they're native to Spain, they're grown around the world now.

- Smoked paprika: Add a hint of earthy smoke to all sorts of dishes without having to light your grill. Once a specialty ingredient, smoked paprika has become more common, and it is sold on the spice aisle at most grocery stores.

- Tuna in olive oil: In Spain, the prized and pricey Ventresca (tuna belly) is most common. Get the same flavors for a fraction of the cost from albacore or all-white tuna packed in olive oil.

Spicy Corn & Crab Chowder

Total cost $10.00

HANDS-ON **35 MIN.**   TOTAL **45 MIN.**   SERVES **4**

Crab claw meat is a darker color than larger, pricier lump. It also has a stronger flavor, which works beautifully in dips and soups like this summer chowder. Poblanos range in heat and are sometimes quite spicy, especially if you're not a fan of fiery flavors. Substitute a red bell pepper or an Anaheim pepper if you want to ensure low-level heat. The portion size on this chowder is ample, close to 2 cups per serving. Serve it for lunch, and you won't need anything to round out the meal.

1 medium poblano chile

2 tablespoons bacon drippings

1 tablespoon butter

³/₄ cup finely chopped onion

1¹/₂ teaspoons kosher salt

¹/₂ teaspoon sugar

¹/₄ teaspoon ground cayenne pepper

3 cups fresh corn kernels (from 4 ears)

1 cup half-and-half, divided

1 pound russet potato, peeled and diced

1³/₄ cups heavy cream

¹/₂ cup bottled clam juice

2 tablespoons all-purpose flour

1 (6.5-ounce) container crab claw meat, shell pieces removed

Freshly ground black pepper

1 green onion, trimmed and thinly vertically sliced

1. Arrange the top rack of the oven 7 inches from the broiler element. Preheat the broiler to high.

2. Place the poblano on a foil-lined baking sheet. Broil 8 minutes on each side or until blackened. Place the pepper in a small paper bag; fold to seal. Let stand 10 minutes. Peel and chop the pepper.

3. Meanwhile, place the drippings and butter in a Dutch oven over medium-high heat; cook until melted. Add the onion and the next 3 ingredients; sauté 4 minutes. Add the corn; sauté 2 minutes. Remove ³/₄ cup corn mixture from the pan, and place in a blender. Add ³/₄ cup half-and-half to the blender; process until smooth.

4. Add the potato to the pan; sauté 1 minute. Stir in the cream and clam juice; bring to a boil. Reduce the heat to medium, and simmer 8 to 10 minutes or until the potato is almost tender, stirring occasionally. Combine the remaining ¹/₄ cup half-and-half and flour in a small bowl, stirring until smooth. Add the flour mixture to the pan. Stir in the corn puree, chopped poblano, and crab; bring to a simmer. Cook for 3 to 5 minutes or until the potatoes are tender, stirring frequently. Adjust the salt and black pepper as needed; sprinkle with the green onion.

Mediterranean Shrimp & Couscous

Total cost $8.96

HANDS-ON 30 MIN.   TOTAL 30 MIN.   SERVES 4

Toast dry Israeli couscous in butter before adding liquid to enhance both the appearance and flavor of this tasty salad. I found the best price on Israeli couscous at Trader Joe's. If you don't have a TJ's, look in the bulk bins at health food stores, Whole Foods, and the like, or you can sub regular couscous. If you do use regular couscous, follow the package directions for rehydrating. Serve this delicious, fresh salad with Smoky Tomato Soup (page 167).

2 tablespoons butter

1 (8-ounce) package Israeli couscous

2 cups Overnight Chicken Stock (page 218) or store-bought

1 tablespoon extra-virgin olive oil

1 teaspoon kosher salt

3/4 teaspoon freshly ground black pepper

12 ounces fresh or frozen unpeeled medium shrimp, thawed, peeled, and deveined

1 large lemon

1 teaspoon Dijon mustard

1/2 teaspoon honey

1/2 teaspoon minced fresh garlic

Pinch of ground cayenne pepper

3 tablespoons canola oil

3/4 cup quartered cherry tomatoes

1/2 cup chopped seeded cucumber

2 tablespoons finely chopped red onion

1 green onion, trimmed and thinly sliced

1. Melt the butter in a medium saucepan over medium-high heat. Add the couscous; cook about 2 minutes or until the couscous is toasted, stirring often. Add the stock to the pan, and bring to a boil. Reduce the heat to medium, and cook 8 to 10 minutes or until the couscous is tender, stirring occasionally. Drain and place the couscous in a large mixing bowl. Toss the hot cooked couscous with the olive oil, 1 teaspoon kosher salt, and the black pepper. Set aside.

2. Cook the shrimp in boiling salted water for 1 to 2 minutes or just until pink. Drain the shrimp; rinse with cold running water. Add the shrimp to the couscous.

3. Grate the zest from the lemon, and place in a small mixing bowl. Squeeze 1/4 cup juice from the lemon through a small sieve into the bowl with the zest. Whisk the mustard and the next 3 ingredients into the juice. Slowly add the canola oil to the bowl, whisking constantly to incorporate. Add the tomatoes, cucumber, and red onion to bowl; toss. Scrape the tomato mixture into the bowl with the couscous mixture; toss. Adjust seasoning as needed. Sprinkle the salad with the sliced green onion.

Ingredient Spotlight: Israeli Couscous

This couscous is more like a distant relative to regular couscous—somewhere between pasta and couscous, in fact. The chewy, puffy grains are sometimes called pearled couscous.

Grilled Shrimp Cobb Salad

Total cost $6.85

HANDS-ON 45 MIN.   TOTAL 45 MIN.   SERVES 4

This recipe is a twist on an American classic, Cobb salad, which generally includes chicken tossed with greens, tomatoes, eggs, blue cheese, bacon, and avocado. I love to use shrimp instead of chicken, and I dress the salad with my tasty Avocado-Ranch Dressing and skip the avocado in the salad. Sub your favorite cheese if you don't like blue cheese.

2 large eggs

Cooking spray

8 ounces peeled and deveined uncooked medium shrimp

5 teaspoons olive oil, divided

1/2 teaspoon kosher salt

2 teaspoons minced fresh flat-leaf parsley

3/4 teaspoon minced fresh garlic

1/2 teaspoon grated fresh lemon zest

Pinch of ground cayenne pepper

8 cups sliced romaine lettuce

1 cup chopped plum tomato

1/4 cup crumbled blue cheese

2 slices bacon, cooked and crumbled

2 green onions, thinly sliced

1/2 cup Avocado-Ranch Dressing (page 214)

1. Bring 2 quarts water to a boil in a saucepan over medium-high heat. Add the eggs to the boiling water; boil 7 minutes. Remove the eggs, and rinse them with cold water. Place the eggs in a bowl of ice water; let stand 10 minutes. Peel the eggs and cut into wedges. Set aside.

2. Heat a grill pan over medium-high heat; coat pan with cooking spray. Toss the shrimp with 1 tablespoon oil, and sprinkle with 1/2 teaspoon salt. Add the shrimp to the pan; cook for 2 minutes on each side or just until the shrimp are opaque. Stir together the remaining 2 teaspoons oil, parsley, garlic, lemon zest, and cayenne in a medium mixing bowl. Add the hot cooked shrimp; toss to coat.

3. Place the lettuce in a large salad bowl; sprinkle the egg wedges, tomatoes, and the next 3 ingredients over lettuce. Top with shrimp, and drizzle with dressing. Season the salad to taste with salt and pepper; toss.

TIGHTWAD TIP
Buying Seafood

Fresh (or fresh-frozen) seafood is pricey, especially if you're paying attention to sustainable fishing practices, as we all should be. The best way to incorporate premium fish and shellfish into budget cooking is to use them sparingly and in combination with more veggies and grains, as I've done in this lively salad.

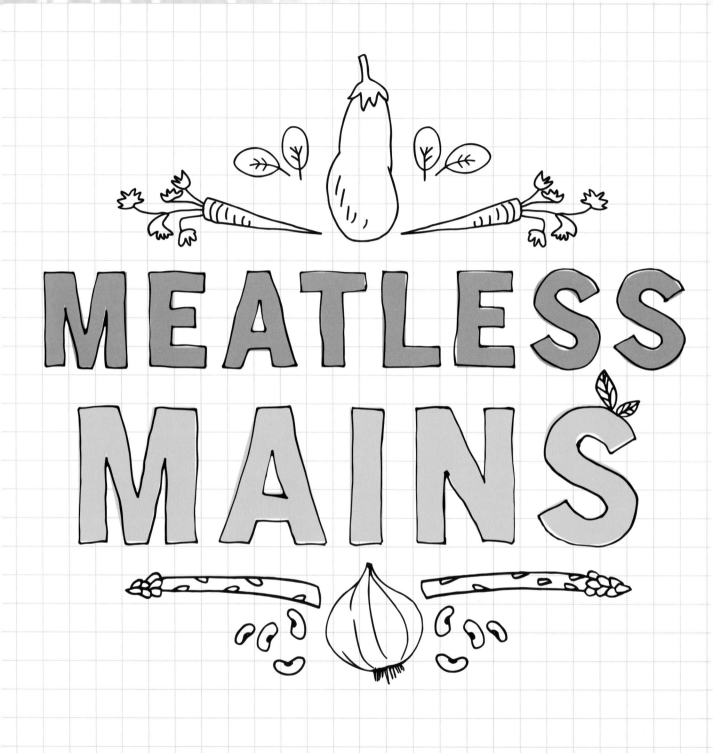

MEATLESS MAINS

Most Americans have historically learned to love and crave meat at the center of our plates. Until the past decade or so, that is. It's not a new idea to go meatless. Much of the world's population eats a vegetarian (or mostly veggie-based) diet for all kinds of reasons. And because that's a fact, there's a world of flavors ripe for the eating. Plants' leaves, roots, fruits, and veggies aside, you need a pantry plentifully stocked with budget-friendly grains, legumes, nuts, and dairy in the fridge, plus other satisfying sources of protein you might otherwise look to meats to supply.

Spring Risotto

HANDS-ON **30 MIN.**   TOTAL **30 MIN.**   SERVES **4**

Total cost **$9.85**

Edamame is a vibrant green soybean, so it adds lots of protein to meatless main dishes like this Italian-style rice. Adding fresh asparagus and goat cheese makes the dish feel worthy of a special occasion, though it's easy and affordable enough to serve on a weeknight. Don't care for goat cheese? No worries, just sub softened cream cheese instead. All you need is a lovely lemony salad to round out the meal.

- 1 pound asparagus, trimmed and cut into $3/4$-inch pieces
- 4 cups Overnight Chicken Stock (page 218) or store-bought
- 2 tablespoons extra-virgin olive oil
- $1^{1}/_{2}$ cups chopped onion
- 3 garlic cloves, minced
- $1^{1}/_{2}$ cups uncooked Arborio rice
- 1 (1-pound) bag frozen shelled edamame
- $1^{1}/_{2}$ teaspoons kosher salt
- 2 ounces goat cheese
- $1/2$ teaspoon freshly ground black pepper
- 1 ounce shaved Parmesan cheese
- 2 teaspoons chopped fresh thyme

TIGHTWAD TIP
Romaine

Buy a whole (untrimmed) head of romaine, and you'll have fresh lettuce left after making this salad. Don't fall for the packages of romaine hearts, or you'll pay way more than you should.

1. Cook the asparagus in boiling salted water for 2 minutes or just until crisp-tender. Drain. Immediately rinse the asparagus with cold running water until the asparagus cools; drain on paper towels.

2. Bring the stock to a simmer in a saucepan; leave over low heat on a back burner. Heat a large saucepan over medium heat. Add the oil to the pan; swirl to coat. Add the onion, and cook for 5 minutes, stirring occasionally. Add the garlic; cook for 2 minutes, stirring constantly. Stir in the rice, edamame, and salt; cook 1 minute, stirring frequently.

3. Stir in 1 cup stock; cook for 4 minutes or until the liquid is nearly absorbed, stirring constantly. Add the remaining stock, $1/2$ cup at a time, stirring constantly until the liquid is absorbed before adding more, about 20 minutes total.

4. Stir in the asparagus, goat cheese, and pepper; cook 1 minute. Sprinkle with the Parmesan cheese and thyme.

SERVE WITH
Romaine & Radish Salad with Lemon Vinaigrette

Place 4 cups torn romaine lettuce, $1/2$ cup quartered radishes, and $1/4$ cup torn fresh mint leaves in a salad bowl. Toss with $1/4$ cup Lemon Vinaigrette (page 213). Season the salad to taste with salt and pepper. Chop $1/2$ avocado, and toss with 1 teaspoon fresh lemon juice. Add to the salad. Toss and serve immediately.

Spicy Stir-Fried Noodles

HANDS-ON 25 MIN.   TOTAL 25 MIN.   SERVES 4

Total cost $9.67

This is a variation on a wildly popular Southeast Asian street food dish. Look for the sweet bean sauce and noodles at Asian markets. The sauce is canned or bottled and the noodles may be frozen. If you can't find them, substitute ramen noodles or dried linguine for lo mein and hoisin for the sweet bean sauce. If you were in Malaysia sampling the dish from a local street vendor, it would be over-the-top spicy. I'm shooting for a mid-level heat with this recipe. Add less chile paste to make a milder version or more to take the heat up a notch. I love the creamy texture of tofu, but if you crave more textural contrast, you can quickly pan-fry it. Serve with Garlic-Chile Roasted Broccoli (page 196).

1 (14-ounce) package water-packed extra-firm tofu, drained

1 (1-pound) package fresh Chinese lo mein egg noodles

3 tablespoons dark sesame oil

5 garlic cloves, minced

$1/2$ teaspoon kosher salt

1 tablespoon sugar

2 tablespoons sambal oelek (ground fresh chile paste)

2 tablespoons fresh lime juice

2 tablespoons sweet bean sauce or hoisin

2 tablespoons soy sauce

4 cups baby spinach

1. Line a plate with a triple layer of paper towels; top with the tofu. Place a triple layer of paper towels on top of the tofu; top with another plate. Let stand for 20 minutes. Cut the tofu into $1/2$-inch cubes.

2. Meanwhile, cook the noodles in a large saucepan of boiling water for 3 minutes or until done; drain in a colander over a bowl, reserving 1 cup cooking liquid. Wipe the pan with paper towels. Heat the oil in pan over medium heat. Add the garlic and salt to the pan; cook for 30 seconds, stirring constantly. Stir in $1/2$ cup reserved cooking liquid; bring to a boil.

3. Combine the sugar and the next 4 ingredients, stirring well; add to the pan with the noodles and the remaining $1/2$ cup cooking liquid. Toss to combine. Stir-fry for 30 seconds or until thoroughly heated, tossing to coat. Remove the pan from the heat. Add the spinach; toss to combine and wilt the spinach. Add the tofu. Serve immediately.

$ TIGHTWAD TIP Use It, Don't Lose It: Sambal Oelek

To use any extra ground fresh chile paste you have on hand, try these options:

- Make spicy aioli with mayo, garlic, and sambal.

- Spice up your homemade pickles.

- Add a kick to a summer mango margarita with just a dab.

- Sour cream + sambal + fresh lime juice = dip or taco topper.

- Add a little heat to hot dogs, roasted Brussels sprouts, or Bloody Marys.

- For a homemade Vietnamese nuoc chom that goes on everything: $1/4$ cup sugar + 2 teaspoons grated fresh lime zest + 2 tablespoons fresh lime juice + 2 tablespoons fish sauce or soy sauce + 1 to 2 teaspoons sambal oelek + $1/4$ teaspoon finely minced fresh garlic.

Butternut Squash Lasagna

Total cost $10.00

HANDS-ON **15 MIN.**   TOTAL **1 HR.**   SERVES **6**

Although this dish is meatless, it's loaded with hearty flavor. Serve with Roasted Green Beans (page 53). The lasagna serves six, so you'll have some leftovers, but the beans serve just four.

5 cups (¹/₂-inch) cubed, seeded butternut squash

2 shallots, sliced into ¹/₄-inch-thick rings

2 tablespoons extra-virgin olive oil

1 tablespoon chopped fresh thyme

1 tablespoon chopped fresh sage

2 tablespoons unsalted butter

3 tablespoons all-purpose flour

1¹/₂ cups Overnight Chicken Stock (page 218) or store-bought

¹/₂ cup whole milk

1¹/₄ cups shredded Swiss cheese, divided

³/₄ cup grated Parmesan cheese, divided

2 teaspoons Dijon mustard

³/₄ teaspoon kosher salt

9 lasagna noodles

Cooking spray

2 tablespoons chopped fresh parsley

1. Preheat the oven to 425°F.

2. Toss the squash and shallots with oil, and arrange in a single layer in a shallow roasting pan. Roast at 425°F for 20 to 22 minutes or until the squash is browned and tender, stirring after 10 minutes. Toss the roasted veggies with the herbs; set aside. Reduce the oven temperature to 400°F.

3. Melt the butter in a small saucepan over medium-high heat. Whisk in the flour; cook 1 minute, whisking constantly. Slowly pour the stock and milk into the pan, whisking constantly; bring to a boil. Cook for 1 to 2 minutes or until the sauce is thickened. Remove from the heat, and let cool for 8 minutes. Stir in ³/₄ cup Swiss cheese, ¹/₄ cup Parmesan, mustard, and salt.

4. Cook the noodles according to the package directions.

5. Spread about ¹/₂ cup sauce in the bottom of an 11- x 7-inch baking dish coated with cooking spray; arrange 3 noodles in a single layer over the sauce. Arrange half of the squash mixture in a single layer on top of the noodles; sprinkle with ¹/₄ cup Swiss and ¹/₄ cup Parmesan. Spread ¹/₃ of the remaining sauce over the top. Repeat the layers once. Arrange the remaining 3 noodles over the sauce; top with the remaining sauce and remaining cheese. Bake at 400°F for 20 minutes or until bubbly and golden on the top. Let stand for 10 minutes before slicing. Sprinkle with parsley.

$ TIGHTWAD TIP Buying Herbs

If you're not growing your own herbs, save money at the grocery store by purchasing a single package of poultry blend herbs. Instead of buying three different packages of fresh herbs, buy just one that contains fresh thyme, sage, and rosemary—some include a couple of sprigs of parsley as well.

"Beefy" Bean Enchiladas

Total cost $9.89

HANDS-ON **1 HR.**   TOTAL **1 HR., 30 MIN.**   SERVES **6**

Don't be intimidated by the ingredient list. This recipe isn't hard to make. It just has a few components, all of which can be prepared in advance. Take note also that the yield is six servings. The leftovers travel well for lunch the next day, and they'll also freeze. In this iteration, I'm using a vegetarian meat substitution, making the dish meatless. When you want a real beefy version, buy 8 ounces ground beef instead of the meat crumbles. Just brown the meat, and continue with the recipe. Serve with Homemade Guacamole & Chips on page 194.

2 dried ancho chiles, stemmed

3 1/2 cups Overnight Chicken Stock (page 218) or store-bought, divided

13 (6-inch) corn tortillas, divided

3 green onions, divided

1/3 cup fresh cilantro leaves

6 teaspoons minced fresh garlic, divided

2 teaspoons olive oil

2 cups chopped onion

1 teaspoon dried Mexican oregano

1/2 teaspoon ground cumin

1/4 teaspoon kosher salt

1 tablespoon tomato paste

1 (15-ounce) can black beans, drained and rinsed

1 1/2 cups meatless ground crumbles (ground beef substitute)

1 tablespoon fresh lime juice

Canola oil

Cooking spray

1 cup shredded sharp cheddar cheese

1/2 cup shredded Monterey Jack cheese

6 tablespoons Mexican crema

1. Preheat the oven to 400°F.

2. Place the ancho chiles in a medium saucepan. Add 3 cups stock; bring to a boil. Reduce the heat, and simmer for 5 minutes. Tear 1 tortilla into pieces, and stir in; simmer for 5 minutes, stirring occasionally. Pour the chile mixture into a blender; let stand for 10 minutes. Coarsely chop 2 green onions. Add the chopped green onions, cilantro, and 2 teaspoons garlic to the blender; process until smooth. Return the mixture to the pan; bring to a boil over medium heat. Cook until reduced to 2 cups, about 7 minutes, stirring occasionally. Remove from the heat.

3. Heat a large skillet over medium-high heat. Add the olive oil to the pan; swirl to coat. Add the onion; cook for 4 minutes or until tender, stirring occasionally. Add the remaining 4 teaspoons garlic, oregano, cumin, and salt; cook for 2 minutes, stirring constantly. Stir in the tomato paste; cook for 1 minute, stirring frequently. Stir in the beans, meatless crumbles, and remaining 1/2 cup broth; bring to a boil. Cook for 1 minute, stirring occasionally. Remove from the heat; stir in the lime juice.

4. Fill a large sauté pan with canola oil to a 2-inch depth; heat over medium heat. Working quickly with 1 tortilla at a time, dip the remaining 12 tortillas in the hot oil for 2 to 3 seconds each or until softened. Drain the softened tortillas on paper towels.

5. Working with 1 softened tortilla at a time, place tortilla on a flat work surface. Spoon about 3 tablespoons of the bean mixture onto 1 end of each tortilla. Roll up, jelly-roll style. Repeat the procedure with the remaining tortillas and bean mixture. Spread 1/2 cup sauce in a 13- x 9-inch baking dish coated with cooking spray. Arrange the tortillas, seam sides down, in the prepared dish. Pour the remaining sauce over the tortillas. Top with the cheeses. Bake at 400°F for 20 minutes or until lightly browned. Let stand 10 minutes. Thinly slice the remaining 1 green onion, and sprinkle on top. Serve with the crema.

Curried Crowder Peas

Total cost
$7.86

HANDS-ON **20 MIN.**   TOTAL **1 HR., 10 MIN.**   SERVES **4**

This meal takes very little prep work, so dinner is a cinch. The peas do take 40 to
50 minutes to tenderize, but that is completely hands-off. Serve with chopped green
onion and lime wedges, if you like, and pair with cornbread for a hearty meatless meal
(cornbread is included in the total cost of the meal). Or serve smaller portions of the peas
as a side dish alongside grilled or roasted meats. Crowder peas are a variety of field pea
that's common in the South and plentiful in that region. Use them if you can find them,
or use your favorite fresh or frozen field peas or canned chickpeas. You can sub fresh or
frozen shell beans like cranberry beans or limas too.

2 tablespoons unsalted butter

1¹/₂ cups finely chopped onion

¹/₂ cup diced carrot

1 tablespoon minced fresh garlic

2 cups shelled fresh crowder peas
   (or other field peas), rinsed

1¹/₄ teaspoons kosher salt

¹/₂ teaspoon freshly ground black
   pepper

¹/₄ teaspoon ground coriander

¹/₄ teaspoon ground dried ginger

Pinch of ground cayenne pepper

Pinch of ground cardamom (optional)

1 cup Overnight Chicken Stock
   (page 218) or store-bought

1 (13.66-ounce) can coconut milk

1 (14.5-ounce) can whole peeled
   tomatoes, drained and crushed
   (about 4 tomatoes)

Melt the butter in a medium Dutch oven over medium-
high heat; swirl to coat. Sauté the onion and carrot in
the hot butter for 3 minutes. Stir in the garlic; sauté for
30 seconds. Add the peas, next 5 ingredients, and the
cardamom, if using; cook for 1 minute, stirring to combine.
Add the stock and remaining ingredients; bring to a boil.
Reduce the heat to medium-low, and simmer 40 to 50
minutes or until the peas are tender, stirring occasionally
and skimming as necessary.

Crowder Peas

A variety of field pea, crowder peas are actually a legume. Common in the
South, they're a little different from black-eyed peas, lady peas, and the
like. Crowders get their name because they're fat and round and crowded
together in the hulls. With a hearty, earthy flavor, these peas are a solid
brown color that gives the pot likker a deep rich color as well.

SANDWICHES, SOUPS & STEWS

SOUP OF THE DAY

Sandwiches don't have to be standard-issue, deli-counter fare. Nevermind ham on rye or turkey on wheat. Get creative. Prosciutto, Pear & Blue Cheese Sandwiches (page 155) meet your budget but taste like you've splurged on a bistro meal. The same principle applies for soups and stews. Both have long been a frugal cook's best friend. Basically a one-pot, one-bowl, complete meal, stew needs little more than crusty bread or salad as accompaniments. It's also the perfect vehicle for making a scrumptious meal from odds and ends (leftover meats, veggie scraps) that might otherwise go to waste, or pantry items already on hand.

Prosciutto, Pear & Blue Cheese Sandwiches

Total cost $8.29

HANDS-ON **20 MIN.**   TOTAL **20 MIN.**   SERVES **4**

Everyone will look forward to sandwich night with offerings like this gorgeous one. In the summer months, you can sub sliced ripe tomatoes or peaches for the pear to make fresh twists on this recipe. Serve with Sweet Potato Wedges on page 202.

8 slices 100% multigrain bread

2 tablespoons butter, softened

2 cups arugula

1 medium shallot, thinly sliced

1 tablespoon extra-virgin olive oil

2 teaspoons red wine vinegar

$1/8$ teaspoon kosher salt

$1/8$ teaspoon freshly ground black pepper

2 ounces thinly sliced prosciutto

1 ripe pear, cored and thinly sliced

1 teaspoon fresh lemon juice

$1/2$ teaspoon honey

2 ounces blue cheese, sliced

1. Arrange the top rack of the oven 5 inches from the broiler element. Preheat the broiler to high.

2. Arrange the bread in a single layer on a baking sheet; broil for 3 minutes or until toasted. Turn the bread slices over; spread the butter evenly over the bread slices. Broil 2 more minutes or until toasted.

3. Combine the arugula and shallot in a medium bowl. Drizzle the arugula mixture with the oil and vinegar; sprinkle with salt and pepper. Toss well to coat. Divide the arugula mixture evenly among 4 bread slices, buttered side up; top evenly with the prosciutto. Toss the pear slices with the juice and honey; divide evenly among sandwiches. Top each sandwich with cheese and 1 bread slice, buttered side down. Halve the sandwiches, and serve immediately.

Got the Blues

There are basically two types of blue cheese, depending on the type of mold used to make the cheese, which mostly determines the overall flavor. If you like your blues strong and stinky, like pungent French Roquefort, for example, look for cheese with deep cavernous holes and dark blue streaks throughout. If you prefer milder, creamier flavors, choose the cheeses with lighter-colored veins with a smoother-looking appearance.

Waffled Grits Sandwiches with Poached Eggs

Total cost $9.56

HANDS-ON **30 MIN.**   TOTAL **30 MIN.**   SERVES **4**

This recipe is based on Slow-Cooker Grits. You'll need 2 cups, and they need to be cold in order to make these waffles successfully. The waffled grits stand in for bread in these open-faced sandwiches. Serve with Asparagus with Pickled Red Onion on page 195. Steam the asparagus and make the pickled onions up to two days ahead, and chill them separately until just before serving.

1 tablespoon distilled white vinegar

5 large eggs, divided

2 cups chilled Slow-Cooker Grits (page 203)

1 cup shredded sharp cheddar cheese

2 slices bacon, cooked and crumbled

2 green onions, trimmed and sliced

Melted butter

2 cups baby spinach

1 cup Marinated Tomatoes (page 209)

1. Preheat the waffle iron to medium-high heat.

2. Fill a straight-sided, 12-inch sauté pan with water to a depth of 2 inches; bring to a simmer over medium-high. Add the vinegar. Reduce the heat to medium. Working with 1 egg at a time, crack the egg into a small bowl; gently slip the egg into the water at the 12:00 position in the pan. Set a timer for 3 minutes. Repeat the procedure 3 times, every 30 seconds, with 3 more eggs, slipping one in the pan at 3:00, another at 6:00, and last at 9:00. Poach each egg for 3 minutes for a soft-cooked center or until the desired degree of doneness, carefully removing each cooked egg with a slotted spoon. Keep warm.

3. Combine the remaining egg and cold grits; stir in the cheese, bacon, and green onions. Brush hot waffle iron with melted butter. Place one-fourth of the grits mixture in the prepared waffle iron. Cook according to the manufacturer's instructions or until the grits are golden and crisp. Repeat with the remaining grits mixture to make a total of 4 waffles.

4. Top each waffle with the spinach and 1 poached egg; season to taste with salt and pepper. Serve with the tomatoes.

Slow-Cooker Chicken Lettuce Cups

Total cost $9.99

HANDS-ON **20 MIN.**   TOTAL **5 HR., 30 MIN.**   SERVES **6**

A super-tasty, all-American twist on lettuce cups, this "sandwich" is perfect for Paleo dieters and others who avoid carbs—and anyone who loves good food. Since the lettuce cups serve six, make this for a casual dinner when company's coming. Or save the leftovers for tomorrow's lunch or later in the week.

1 small yellow onion, cut into wedges

1 small Granny Smith apple, cut into wedges

6 garlic cloves, smashed

4 uncooked thick slices bacon, chopped

1 (4-pound) whole chicken

6 tablespoons cider vinegar, divided

1/2 cup mayonnaise

1/8 teaspoon ground cayenne pepper

6 lettuce leaves

Garnishes:

1/2 to 1 cup spicy bread and butter pickles

3 green onions, sliced

1 bell pepper, sliced

1. Place the first 4 ingredients in a 7-quart slow cooker. Add the chicken, 1/3 cup vinegar, and 1/2 cup water. Sprinkle the chicken with salt and black pepper. Cover and cook on LOW for 5 to 6 hours or until the chicken is done and pulls easily from the bone. Remove the chicken from the slow cooker, reserving the cooking liquid; let stand for 15 minutes. Pull the chicken from the bones, discarding the skin; reserve the bones to make stock. Shred the chicken.

2. Pour the cooking liquid through a fine wire-mesh strainer into a measuring cup; discard the solids. Let the cooking liquid stand for 10 minutes. Skim the fat, and reserve 1/3 cup cooking liquid. Toss the remaining cooking liquid with the shredded chicken.

3. Whisk together the mayonnaise, cayenne, reserved 1/3 cup cooking liquid, and remaining 1 1/2 teaspoons vinegar; season to taste with salt and pepper. Spoon the chicken into the lettuce leaves; drizzle with the sauce. Top with desired garnishes.

SERVE WITH

Sesame Noodles

Cook 8 ounces of spaghetti according to the package directions; drain. Toss the hot cooked noodles with 2 tablespoons dark sesame oil. Season to taste with salt and pepper. Serve immediately.

Southern-Style Chicken Biscuit Sandwiches

Total cost
$9.03

HANDS-ON 1 HR.   TOTAL 2 HR., 30 MIN.   SERVES 4

Go ahead and earmark this page now. You'll use this biscuit recipe every time you need to make some. This recipe yields only four big, fluffy biscuits, but you can easily double or triple the recipe if you need more. The yummy sauce has a generous yield, so you may have some left over. It's great to use as a marinade for grilled chicken or pork. Get all organized before you start cooking, so you can power through with ease. Serve with carrot and celery sticks with Ranch dressing and grapes.

CHICKEN

Pecan-Crusted Chicken (page 49)

SAUCE

1¼ cups cider vinegar

⅓ cup finely chopped onion

3 tablespoons ketchup

1½ teaspoons minced fresh garlic

1 teaspoon kosher salt

¾ teaspoon Dijon mustard

½ teaspoon garlic powder

½ teaspoon Worcestershire sauce

¼ teaspoon Louisiana-style hot sauce

1 tablespoon butter

⅛ teaspoon freshly ground black pepper

BISCUITS

Biscuits (recipe at right)

ADDITIONAL INGREDIENTS

Onion slices

Dill pickle chips

1. Prepare the chicken.

2. To prepare the sauce, combine the cider vinegar and the next 8 ingredients in a small saucepan; bring to a boil over medium-high heat, stirring occasionally. Reduce the heat to medium; simmer for 8 to 10 minutes or until mixture reaches a syrupy consistency, stirring often. Remove from the heat; whisk in 1 tablespoon butter and black pepper. Cool for 5 minutes. Place mixture in a blender; process until smooth.

3. Prepare the biscuits.

4. To assemble, spoon half of the sauce into a shallow dish; add the Pecan-Crusted Chicken to the dish. Turn the chicken over to coat. Split the biscuits in half. Place 1 piece of chicken on each biscuit bottom; top with onion slices and pickles. Drizzle on more sauce, if desired, and place a biscuit top on each. Serve with the remaining sauce or reserve for another use.

Biscuits

1. Preheat the oven to 450°F. Combine 1¼ cups self-rising soft wheat flour (such as White Lily), 1 teaspoon kosher salt, and ½ teaspoon sugar. Cut 2 tablespoons cold butter into small pieces. Cut in the cold butter and 1 tablespoon vegetable shortening with a pastry blender or 2 knives until the mixture resembles coarse sand. Make a well in the center of the flour mixture, and pour 3 tablespoons heavy cream and 6 tablespoons whole buttermilk into the well. Stir until a moist shaggy dough forms.

2. Turn the dough out onto a lightly floured surface, and gently pat the dough into a 6- x 4-inch rectangle that is ½ inch thick. Fold the top third of the dough down over the middle. Then fold the bottom third of the dough over the flap of the top third. Rotate the dough a quarter turn; gently pat the dough, lengthwise, into a rectangle. Repeat the folding and patting processes twice more, ending with the folding step. The dough should be 6 x 4 inches and ¾ inch thick. Cut the dough into 4 (3- x 2-inch) rectangles. Line the bottom of an 8-inch square pan with parchment paper; coat with cooking spray. Arrange the dough in the pan. Bake at 450°F for 15 to 20 minutes or until the biscuits are golden. Brush the tops of the warm biscuits with 1 tablespoon melted butter.

Kung Pao Chicken Tacos

Total cost
$9.96

HANDS-ON **30 MIN.**   TOTAL **1 HR.**   SERVES **4**

Your family will love the mash-up of a Tex-Mex taco stuffed with peanutty Chinese-style chicken. So fresh and fantastic. Serve the tacos with Caramelized Pineapple & Avocado Salad (page 194) and chips.

6 skinless, boneless chicken thighs, cut into bite-sized pieces

1/4 cup lower-sodium soy sauce, divided

2 tablespoons dark sesame oil, divided

2 tablespoons honey, divided

6 tablespoons cornstarch, divided

1/2 teaspoon kosher salt

2 tablespoons canola oil, divided

2 teaspoons rice vinegar

1 teaspoon sambal oelek (ground fresh chile paste)

1 large garlic clove, minced

3 tablespoons coarsely chopped dry-roasted peanuts

3/4 cup diagonally sliced celery (about 2 ribs)

8 (6-inch) corn tortillas

1/2 medium-sized red bell pepper, thinly sliced

2 green onions, trimmed and thinly diagonally sliced

4 lime wedges

1. Place the chicken in a large ziplock plastic bag. Whisk together 2 tablespoons soy sauce, 1 tablespoon sesame oil, and 1 1/2 teaspoons honey in a small bowl. Add the soy mixture to the bag with the chicken; seal. Marinate at room temperature for 30 minutes, turning the bag over after 15 minutes. Remove the chicken from the bag; discard the marinade.

2. Place 1/3 cup cornstarch in a shallow dish. Sprinkle the chicken evenly with salt. Dredge the chicken in cornstarch; shake off excess. Heat a large skillet over medium-high heat. Add 1 tablespoon canola oil to the pan; swirl to coat. Add half of the coated chicken to the pan; sauté for 6 minutes or until done, turning to brown on all sides. Remove the chicken from the pan using a slotted spoon; drain on paper towels. Repeat the procedure with the remaining 1 tablespoon canola oil and coated chicken.

3. Whisk together the remaining 2 tablespoons soy sauce and 1 1/2 teaspoons cornstarch in a large microwave-safe bowl. Add the remaining 1 tablespoon sesame oil, 1 1/2 teaspoons honey, vinegar, and sambal oelek; whisk until well blended. Microwave at HIGH for 1 1/2 minutes or until slightly thick, stirring twice. Stir in the garlic. Add the chicken, peanuts, and celery to bowl with the sauce; toss.

4. Heat the tortillas according to the package directions, or toast under the broiler until lightly blistered. Divide the chicken filling evenly among the warm tortillas; top the tacos with bell pepper and green onions; serve with lime wedges.

Carrot-Apple Soup

HANDS-ON **25 MIN.**   TOTAL **1 HR., 25 MIN.**   SERVES **4**

Total cost
$9.73

You won't believe the amazing fresh carrot flavor and pale hue of this refreshing soup. Both are possible because you simply boil the ingredients together until they're soft. This soup is perfect for a starter to a fancy meal, but it's equally delicious as a side to any roasted or grilled meat. It's also magnificent paired with a humble ham and cheese sandwich. Plan ahead if serving with the DIY Crème Fraîche, which takes a day to make.

1½ pounds carrots, peeled and chopped (about 8 large)

1 pound Granny Smith apples, peeled and chopped (about 2 large)

1 large yellow onion, chopped

2 cups heavy whipping cream

1½ cups Overnight Chicken Stock (page 218) or store-bought

1¼ cups apple cider

3 fresh thyme sprigs

1 teaspoon kosher salt

½ teaspoon freshly ground black pepper

DIY Crème Fraîche (page 101) or sour cream

Ingredient Spotlight: Apple Cider

Unlike products called juice or juice beverage, cider should be 100% pure unfiltered, unsweetened nectar of the fruit. Read package labels to be sure you're getting the real deal. Trader Joe's makes Honey Crisp Apple Cider, the best product you're likely to find unless you're buying directly from a local orchard (2 quarts, $2.99).

1. Bring all ingredients except crème fraîche to a boil in a Dutch oven over medium-high heat; reduce the heat to low, and simmer, stirring occasionally, about 45 minutes or until the carrots are tender. Remove from the heat, and cool 15 minutes.

2. Remove the thyme sprigs. Process the soup, in batches, in a blender or food processor until smooth. (For a thinner soup, you can stir in more broth, 1 tablespoon at a time.) Ladle the soup into individual bowls; top with the pepper and drizzle with crème fraîche, and serve immediately.

SERVE WITH
French-Style Ham & Cheese

Slice 1 (1-pound) French bread baguette in half lengthwise; spread 2 tablespoons soft butter over the bottom half of the bread. Top with 8 paper-thin slices of prosciutto and 1.5 ounces of thinly sliced Gruyère cheese. Place the top half of the baguette on the cheese; cut into 4 sandwiches.

Smoky Tomato Soup

HANDS-ON **10 MIN.**   TOTAL **45 MIN.**   SERVES **4**

Beyond simple to make, this soup is creamy, silky, and delicious. Pair it with Goat Cheese Toasts or grilled cheese sandwiches for a perfect lunch. For dinner, make Roasted Chickpeas on page 206, and pile them on top of each serving. (The menu cost includes soup and Roasted Chickpeas.)

Total cost $9.15

2 red bell peppers, halved lengthwise

2 tablespoons olive oil

6 garlic cloves, smashed

1 cup Overnight Chicken Stock (page 218) or store-bought

3/4 cup heavy whipping cream

2 (28-ounce) cans no-salt-added whole peeled tomatoes, undrained and crushed

1/2 medium-sized yellow onion, coarsely chopped

3/4 teaspoon smoked paprika

1 1/2 teaspoons salt

1/4 teaspoon ground cayenne pepper

2 tablespoons fresh flat-leaf parsley

2 tablespoons sliced almonds, toasted

1. Arrange the top rack of the oven 5 inches from the broiler element. Preheat the broiler to high.

2. Discard the seeds and membranes from the bell peppers; place, skin sides up, on a foil-lined baking sheet. Broil for 8 minutes or until blackened. Seal in a paper bag; let stand for 10 minutes. Peel.

3. Heat the oil in a saucepan over medium heat; swirl to coat. Add the garlic; cook for 1 minute. Add the stock, cream, tomatoes, and onion, and bring to a simmer. Add the paprika, salt, and cayenne; simmer for 20 minutes, stirring occasionally. Cool for 10 minutes. Place the tomato mixture and bell pepper in a blender; puree. Season to taste with salt and pepper. Ladle the soup into bowls; sprinkle with the parsley and almonds.

SERVE WITH
Goat Cheese Toasts

Halve 2 slices sourdough bread diagonally; brush with 1 tablespoon melted butter. Broil for 2 minutes or until toasted. Spread 2 ounces goat cheese over the toasts; broil 1 more minute or until the cheese browns lightly. Sprinkle with salt.

South American Shrimp Stew

Total cost
$10.00

HANDS-ON **25 MIN.**   TOTAL **50 MIN.**   SERVES **4**

The combination of tomatoes, slightly sweet coconut milk, and tangy fresh lime juice is delicious in this hearty seafood stew.

12 ounces frozen medium shrimp unpeeled, thawed

2 tablespoons extra-virgin olive oil, divided

1 tablespoon tomato paste

1 large carrot, peeled and sliced (about ½ cup)

1 celery rib, sliced (about ⅓ cup)

1½ cups chopped yellow onion (1 medium onion)

1 cup chopped red bell pepper (about 1 medium pepper)

2 teaspoons chopped fresh garlic

¾ teaspoon crushed red pepper

1 (14.5-ounce) can whole peeled tomatoes, drained and crushed

1 (15-ounce) can unsweetened coconut milk

1¼ teaspoons kosher salt

¼ teaspoon freshly ground black pepper

8 ounces skinless halibut fillet, cut into 1-inch pieces

½ cup chopped green onions

3 tablespoons fresh lime juice

1. Peel and devein the shrimp; reserve the shrimp shells. Heat a medium saucepan over medium-high heat. Add 1 tablespoon oil to the pan; swirl to coat. Stir in the shrimp shells and tomato paste; sauté until fragrant, about 1 minute, stirring constantly. Add the carrot, celery, and 2 cups water; bring to a boil. Reduce the heat to medium-low; simmer until reduced to about 1½ cups, about 15 to 20 minutes, stirring occasionally. Strain the shrimp stock through a fine-mesh sieve; discard the solids. Wipe the pan with paper towels.

2. Return the pan to medium-high. Add the remaining 1 tablespoon oil; swirl to coat. Stir in the onion and bell pepper; sauté for about 6 minutes or until the onion is tender, stirring often. Stir in the garlic and crushed red pepper; sauté 1 minute, stirring constantly. Add the shrimp stock, tomatoes, coconut milk, salt, and pepper; bring to a boil, stirring occasionally. Reduce the heat to medium-low, and simmer until the flavors meld, about 15 to 20 minutes, stirring occasionally. Stir in the shrimp and fish; cook until the seafood is opaque and cooked through, about 3 minutes. Remove from the heat. Stir in the green onions and lime juice. Taste and adjust the seasoning as needed.

TIGHTWAD TIP
Buying Shrimp

Be sure to buy shrimp in the shells, so you can make a quick shrimp stock to really reinforce the shrimp flavor. Besides, it's more expensive to buy shrimp that's already peeled and deveined.

Old School Chicken & Dumplings

Total cost $8.86

HANDS-ON **55 MIN.**   TOTAL **2 HR., 55 MIN.**   SERVES **4**

This generous serving of soup is chock-full of vegetables, so it's hearty enough to serve as a complete meal if you don't want to bother with a side. But a Wilted Spinach Salad (page 31) pairs perfectly with this comfort-food classic, and it's included in the menu cost.

BROTH

1 tablespoon whole black peppercorns

4 chicken leg quarters, skinned

3 celery ribs, sliced

2 medium carrots, peeled and sliced

2 bay leaves

1 large onion, peeled and cut into 8 wedges

DUMPLINGS

1 cup all-purpose flour (about 4.5 ounces), divided

1 teaspoon baking powder

1/4 teaspoon salt

1/4 cup chilled butter, cut into small pieces

3 tablespoons buttermilk

REMAINING INGREDIENTS

Cooking spray

1 1/2 cups chopped onion

1 cup thinly sliced celery

3/4 cup (1/4-inch-thick) slices carrot

3/4 teaspoon salt

1 tablespoon all-purpose flour

2 tablespoons finely chopped fresh chives

1. To prepare the broth, combine 12 cups cold water, peppercorns, and next 5 ingredients in a large stockpot; bring to a boil. Reduce the heat to medium-low; simmer 2 hours, skimming as necessary. Remove the chicken from the broth; cool. Remove the meat from the bones. Shred the meat; set aside. Discard the bones. Strain the broth through a sieve over a bowl; discard solids. Place the broth in a large saucepan; bring to a boil. Cook until reduced to 6 cups, about 8 minutes.

2. To prepare the dumplings, weigh or lightly spoon flour into a dry measuring cup; level with a knife. Combine 3/4 cup flour, baking powder, and 1/4 teaspoon salt; whisk. Cut in the butter with a pastry blender or 2 knives until the mixture resembles coarse meal. Add the buttermilk; stir to combine. Turn the dough out onto a lightly floured surface; knead 5 times, adding the remaining 1/4 cup flour as needed. Divide the mixture into 24 equal portions.

3. Heat a large Dutch oven over medium-high heat. Coat the pan with cooking spray. Add the chopped onion, 1 cup celery, and 3/4 cup carrot to the pan; sauté for 4 minutes, stirring occasionally. Add the broth and 3/4 teaspoon salt; bring to a boil. Reduce the heat, and simmer for 20 minutes or until the vegetables are tender. Drop the dumplings into the pan; cover and cook for 10 minutes or until the dumplings are done, stirring occasionally. Remove 1/4 cup liquid from the pan; stir in 1 tablespoon flour. Return the chicken to the pan. Add the flour mixture to the pan; bring to a boil. Cook for 1 minute or until slightly thickened, stirring occasionally. Remove from the heat; stir in the chives.

TIGHTWAD TIP
Double Duty

Keep your budget in check and pump up the flavor of this comfort-food classic by cooking your chicken and making stock at the same time.

Cajun-Style Chicken & Sausage Gumbo

Total cost
$9.40

HANDS-ON **30 MIN.**   TOTAL **1 HR., 15 MIN.**   SERVES **6**

Gumbo doesn't normally have carrots in it, but I like to use them to add color to this hearty, flavor-filled dish. If you make this in the summer, use fresh okra. In the fall, winter, and spring, use frozen sliced okra, and it's still super yummy and affordable.

2 tablespoons extra-virgin olive oil

3 bone-in, skin-on chicken leg quarters

2³/₄ teaspoons kosher salt, divided

¹/₄ teaspoon freshly ground black pepper

2 cups diced smoked sausage (about 12 ounces)

2 tablespoons tomato paste

2 cups chopped onion (from 1 large)

1 cup chopped carrot

1 green bell pepper, trimmed, seeded, and chopped (about 1 cup)

³/₄ cup chopped celery (about 2 ribs)

2 tablespoons minced fresh garlic

³/₄ teaspoon ground cumin

¹/₄ teaspoon ground cayenne pepper

¹/₄ cup unsalted butter

¹/₄ cup all-purpose flour

4 cups Overnight Chicken Stock (page 218) or store-bought

2 cups sliced fresh or frozen okra

2 teaspoons chopped fresh thyme leaves

2 cups hot cooked rice

3 green onions, trimmed and thinly diagonally sliced (about ¹/₂ cup)

Hot sauce (optional)

1. Heat a Dutch oven over medium-high heat. Add the oil to the pan; swirl to coat. Sprinkle the chicken with ³/₄ teaspoon of the salt and pepper. Add the chicken to the pan; sauté for 3 to 5 minutes on each side to brown. Remove the chicken from the pan, reserving 1 tablespoon drippings in the pan; set the chicken aside.

2. Add the sausage to the pan; cook, stirring frequently, until the sausage begins to brown, 3 to 4 minutes. Stir in the tomato paste; cook for 1 minute, stirring constantly. Add the onion, carrot, bell pepper, and celery; cook until softened, about 4 minutes, stirring often. Stir in garlic, cumin, and cayenne; cook for 30 seconds, stirring constantly. Remove the sausage mixture from the pan.

3. Melt the butter in the pan over medium-high heat. Add the flour and remaining 2 teaspoons salt; whisk until smooth. Cook until the roux turns a deep amber color, whisking often, about 4 minutes. Return the sausage mixture to the pan; stir well to combine. Slowly add the stock to the pan, whisking constantly. Return the chicken to the pan, and bring the mixture to a boil. Reduce the heat to medium-low, and simmer gently for about 35 minutes or until the chicken is done. Using a pair of tongs, carefully remove the chicken from the pan; let the chicken stand at room temperature for 10 minutes. Pull the meat from the bones; shred the chicken. Discard the bones and skin.

4. Stir the shredded chicken, okra, and thyme into the gumbo; cook until slightly thickened and okra is tender, 2 to 4 minutes, stirring occasionally. Remove from the heat. Ladle the gumbo over rice; garnish with green onions and, if desired, hot sauce.

Slow-Cooker Mexican Stew

Total cost $9.56

HANDS-ON **30 MIN.**   TOTAL **7 HR., 40 MIN.**   SERVES **4**

Classic posole, a delicious slow-simmered Mexican pork stew, is often reserved for special occasions because it's a time-consuming labor of love. But this one gives you all the comfort and flavor of the classic version, conveniently made in your slow cooker. This traditional red posole yields enough for four generous servings. In a pinch, you could probably serve five. Make a double batch to feed a crowd, or if you want to freeze some for later.

1 tablespoon olive oil

12 ounces boneless pork shoulder (Boston butt), cut into 1/2-inch cubes

1 cup chopped white onion

1/2 cup chopped carrot

1 1/2 teaspoons ground cumin

1 teaspoon kosher salt

1/2 teaspoon black pepper

1/4 teaspoon ground cayenne pepper

3 garlic cloves, coarsely chopped

1 (29-ounce) can hominy, drained and rinsed

1 (14.5-ounce) can crushed tomatoes

2 cups Overnight Chicken Stock (page 218) or store-bought, divided

1 dried ancho chile

2 cups thinly sliced cabbage

1/2 cup thinly sliced radishes

2 green onions, thinly sliced

1 jalapeño chile, thinly sliced

1 avocado, peeled, pitted, and sliced

1/2 lime, cut into wedges

1. Heat a large skillet over medium-high heat. Add the oil to the pan; swirl to coat. Add the pork to the pan; sauté 6 minutes. Place the pork in a 5-quart slow cooker. Stir the onion, next 8 ingredients, and 1 1/2 cups stock into the slow cooker with the pork. Microwave the remaining 1/2 cup stock in a microwave-safe bowl on HIGH for 3 minutes or until boiling. Add the dried chile, and let stand for 10 minutes.

2. Remove and discard the top of the chile. Place the chile and soaking liquid in a blender; process until smooth. Stir the chile mixture into the pork mixture. Cover and cook on LOW for 7 to 8 hours or until the pork is very tender. Serve with the cabbage, radishes, green onions, jalapeño, avocado, and lime wedges.

TIGHTWAD TIP
Do It Yourself

Buy a whole head of regular green cabbage and slice it yourself. Napa and specialty varieties are more expensive.

Winter Squash & Chickpea Stew

HANDS-ON **20 MIN.**   TOTAL **10 HR., 30 MIN.**   SERVES **8**

The combo of all these warm spices with briny olives and sweet raisins is Moroccan-inspired, so serving the stew over couscous makes perfect sense. You'll get a large yield, so make a batch when you need to feed a crowd, or freeze half for later. If you do freeze some for later, you'll only need half as much couscous.

Total cost $6.53

1 cup dried chickpeas

1 tablespoon olive oil

1¹/₂ cups chopped onion

5 garlic cloves, minced

1 tablespoon tomato paste

1¹/₂ teaspoons ground cumin

1 teaspoon kosher salt

¹/₂ teaspoon ground cayenne pepper

¹/₂ teaspoon ground cinnamon

¹/₄ teaspoon ground turmeric

3 cups Overnight Chicken Stock (page 218) or store-bought

²/₃ cup sliced pimiento-stuffed olives

¹/₂ cup golden raisins

1 (28-ounce) can whole tomatoes, undrained and crushed

4 cups chopped peeled butternut squash

1 cup frozen green peas, thawed

6 cups hot cooked couscous

Chopped fresh cilantro leaves (optional)

1. Bring 2 quarts water to a boil in a medium saucepan over medium-high heat. Add the chickpeas; boil 2 minutes. Remove from the heat. Cover and let stand for 1 hour; drain. Place the beans in a 6-quart slow cooker.

2. Heat a large skillet over medium-high heat. Add the oil to the pan; swirl to coat. Sauté the onion in the hot oil for 4 minutes, stirring occasionally. Add the garlic; sauté for 1 minute, stirring constantly. Stir in the tomato paste and the next 5 ingredients; sauté for 30 seconds, stirring constantly. Add the onion mixture to the slow cooker. Add the stock and the next 3 ingredients to the slow cooker; cover and cook on HIGH for 8 hours.

3. Add the squash to the slow cooker. Cover and cook on HIGH for 1 hour; stir in the peas. Serve over couscous. Sprinkle with cilantro, if desired.

Smoky Turkey & Sweet Potato Chili

Total cost $9.99

HANDS-ON **30 MIN.**   TOTAL **8 HR., 30 MIN.**   SERVES **9**

Chipotle chiles add a kick, but sweet potatoes balance the heat. Adjust the spice in this homey chili by increasing or decreasing the amount of chipotle to suit your taste. Buy the large dried lima beans if you can find them. They really look amazing and also give the chili a decidedly Southern accent. If you don't find the big ones, regular limas or butter beans will work just the same. Notice the large yield on this recipe—and still less than $10. Wow! The leftovers will freeze.

1¼ pounds ground turkey

3½ teaspoons kosher salt, divided

¾ teaspoon black pepper, divided

2 tablespoons olive oil

1 tablespoon tomato paste

1 cup Mexican beer

1 cup dried pinto beans

1½ tablespoons chopped canned chipotle peppers in adobo sauce

2 teaspoons ground cumin

1 teaspoon smoked paprika

2 medium-sized green bell peppers, coarsely chopped

1 (8-ounce) package dried lima beans

1 large onion, coarsely chopped

5 cups Overnight Chicken Stock (page 218) or store-bought

2½ cups (½-inch) peeled sweet potato cubes

1 teaspoon grated fresh lime zest

½ teaspoon fresh lime juice

¼ cup sour cream

1 small ripe avocado, peeled, pitted, and chopped

1. Season the turkey with ½ teaspoon kosher salt and ¼ teaspoon black pepper. Heat the oil in a large skillet over medium-high heat; swirl to coat. Add the turkey to the pan, and cook for 4 minutes or until browned. Transfer the mixture to a 6-quart slow cooker.

2. Add the tomato paste to the pan, and cook, stirring often, 30 seconds. Add the beer, and bring to a boil, stirring to loosen the browned bits from the bottom of the pan. Boil for 2 to 3 minutes or until reduced by half; stir into the turkey mixture. Add the beans and the next 6 ingredients; stir in the stock. Cover and cook on HIGH for 7 hours. Stir in the sweet potatoes; cover and cook on HIGH for 1 hour or until the potatoes are tender. Adjust the seasoning with salt and pepper as needed. Stir the zest and juice into the sour cream; top each serving with the sour cream mixture and avocado.

Chipotle Pepper in Adobo

Chipotle peppers are smoked jalapeño chiles that are canned in mild, tangy, slightly sweet red sauce. Use a little in all kinds of recipes to add an earthy, smoky, mildly spicy note that provides depth. If you're looking for fiery hot, just add more.

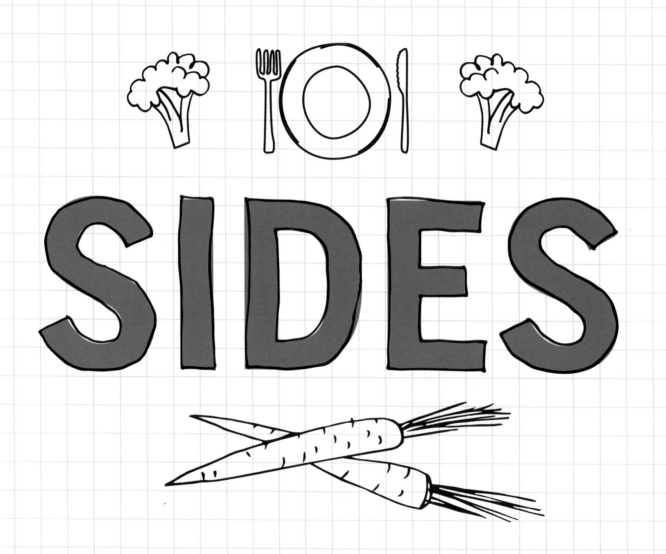

SIDES

Side dishes are prime territory for penny-pinching, partly because you can use low-cost grains and produce. Starchy sides like Potato Smashers (page 200) and Browned Butter Rice Pilaf (page 203) add rib-sticking satisfaction to lighter entrées, while veggie-based sides like Snap Pea Slaw (page 189) and Lemon & Mint Veggie Salad (page 184) are just the thing to pair with hearty mains. When you pair a side with a main, consider how the flavors will taste together, but also think about texture variety: Creamy pastas, fork-tender meats, and delicate fish all cry out for the crunch of a fresh slaw or salad.

Winter Salad with Grapefruit Vinaigrette

Total cost $4.01

HANDS-ON **20 MIN.**   TOTAL **20 MIN.**   SERVES **4**

This is a colorful salad that would be great as a side at a brunch party. The grapefruit is tart and slightly bitter, which balances out the sweetness of the honey and pear. Make this "your own" by using whatever greens you have on hand. There's ample dressing for the salad, possibly more than you'll need. Keep any extra in the fridge—you can use it on salad or toss it with plain steamed veggies.

4 cups sliced romaine lettuce

¹/₂ cup thinly sliced radishes (about 4 radishes)

¹/₄ cup thinly vertically sliced red onion (from 1 small onion)

1 ripe pear, cored and sliced

¹/₄ cup freshly squeezed grapefruit juice (from 1 grapefruit)

4 teaspoons fresh lemon juice

¹/₂ teaspoon kosher salt

¹/₄ teaspoon freshly ground black pepper

2 teaspoons honey

1 teaspoon Dijon mustard

¹/₈ teaspoon vanilla extract

1 tablespoon extra-virgin olive oil

1 tablespoon canola oil

1. Place the lettuce in a salad bowl; top with the radishes, onion, and pear.

2. Combine the grapefruit juice, lemon juice, salt, and pepper in a small bowl. Whisk in the honey, mustard, and vanilla. Slowly drizzle the oils into the grapefruit juice mixture, whisking constantly to emulsify. Drizzle the dressing over the salad; toss.

Lemon & Mint Veggie Salad

Total cost
$3.97

HANDS-ON **20 MIN.**   TOTAL **20 MIN.**   SERVES **4**

As far as sides go, this pretty shaved salad is on the pricey side, so let it shine by pairing it with fairly plain roasted or grilled meats. Or chop a couple of grilled chicken breasts and toss them into the salad to create a fresh twist on the trusty old chicken salad.

2 tablespoons fresh lemon juice

1 tablespoon sugar

$1/2$ teaspoon Dijon mustard

$1/2$ teaspoon minced fresh garlic

$3/4$ teaspoon kosher salt, divided

$1/4$ teaspoon freshly ground black
   pepper, divided

2 tablespoons olive oil

4 teaspoons canola oil

1 large Granny Smith apple, cored and
   julienne cut

2 cups shaved seeded cucumber

$1/4$ cup small fresh mint leaves,
   coarsely chopped

1 medium zucchini, shaved

4 green onions, trimmed and thinly
   diagonally sliced

Whisk together the lemon juice, sugar, mustard, garlic, $1/4$ teaspoon salt, and $1/8$ teaspoon pepper in a large bowl. Slowly drizzle the oils into the juice mixture, whisking constantly until blended. Add the apple; toss to coat. Add the cucumber and the next 3 ingredients. Sprinkle the salad with the remaining $1/2$ teaspoon salt and $1/8$ teaspoon pepper; toss.

 TIGHTWAD TIP
Mint

If you plant nothing else, try growing fresh mint. It's hearty and thrives with almost no maintenance required.

Celery-Apple Salad

Total cost
$2.87

HANDS-ON **10 MIN.**   TOTAL **10 MIN.**   SERVES **4**

So simple, yet so delicious and fresh—and crunchy. This salad is great with plain-ish grilled or roasted chicken, pork, or fish. And it's an absolute snap to pull together.

2 tablespoons fresh lemon juice

½ teaspoon sugar

¼ teaspoon kosher salt

¼ teaspoon freshly ground black pepper

2 cups thinly sliced Honeycrisp apple

2 cups sliced celery

⅓ cup thinly vertically sliced red onion

2 tablespoons extra-virgin olive oil

½ cup loosely packed fresh flat-leaf parsley leaves

Whisk together the first 4 ingredients in a medium bowl. Add the apple; toss to coat. Stir in the celery and onion; toss. Drizzle with the oil. Add the parsley; toss.

 TIGHTWAD TIP
Buying Apples, Part II

I mentioned elsewhere in the book (page 103) to avoid buying Honeycrisp apples because they're usually one of, if not the most, expensive apples. But they make this salad a standout. If you like the sound of this side but need to lower the costs, sub another apple in place of Honeycrisp. Of course, you can use any apple you like, so choose your favorite. I prefer red-skinned apples for the color contrast and ones with plenty of sweet-tart flavor like Pink Lady.

Snap Pea Slaw

HANDS-ON 15 MIN.　TOTAL 15 MIN.　SERVES 4

Make this nontraditional slaw stand out by slicing the sugar snaps thinly and diagonally across the pod. Serve with fish, chicken, or anything really. Make the flavor profile more neutral by subbing extra-virgin olive oil for the sesame oil, if you prefer.

Total cost
$1.43

2 cups sugar snap peas, trimmed and thinly diagonally sliced

$1/2$ cup grated radishes

$1/4$ cup very thinly vertically sliced shallots

1 tablespoon dark sesame oil

2 teaspoons rice vinegar

$1/4$ teaspoon kosher salt

Combine the peas, radishes, and shallots in a large salad bowl. Combine the oil and vinegar; drizzle over the pea mixture. Sprinkle with the salt; toss.

Tropical Cabbage Crunch Slaw

Total cost $3.67

HANDS-ON **20 MIN.**   TOTAL **30 MIN.**   SERVES **4**

Pineapples are best during winter months, so you can turn to this retro slaw to brighten your dreariest days. Or since mangoes are best in the warmer months, you can serve it alongside grilled meats, like Lemon-Soy Grilled Chicken (page 54) or a rack of ribs. If you want to prep ahead, you can assemble the slaw, but toss in the noodles and almonds just before serving, so they'll stay nice and crunchy.

2 cups thinly sliced green cabbage

¼ cup thinly vertically sliced red onion

¾ teaspoon kosher salt

¾ teaspoon grated fresh lime zest

1 ½ tablespoons fresh lime juice

2 tablespoons light brown sugar

⅛ teaspoon ground cayenne pepper

⅔ cup chopped cored fresh pineapple

½ peeled, pitted, chopped fresh mango

1 ½ tablespoons coconut oil, melted

1 ½ teaspoons canola oil

¾ teaspoon distilled white vinegar

1 teaspoon granulated sugar

1 (3-ounce) package ramen noodles (such as Maruchan), crushed

¼ cup toasted sliced almonds

1. Place the cabbage and red onion in a large mixing bowl; sprinkle with the salt. Whisk together the zest and the next 3 ingredients in a medium bowl. Add the pineapple and mango; let stand 10 minutes. Add the pineapple mixture to the cabbage mixture.

2. Combine the coconut oil and the next 3 ingredients, whisking until the sugar dissolves. Pour the coconut mixture over the cabbage mixture; toss. Add the noodles to the slaw; discard the seasoning packet. Toss to combine. Season to taste with salt and pepper; toss. Sprinkle with the almonds, and serve immediately.

TIGHTWAD TIP
Coconut Oil

If you have coconut oil on hand, this is a great place to use it to amp up the tropical flavors in this refreshing slaw. If you don't have coconut oil, sub canola oil instead.

Jicama & Bell Pepper Slaw

Total cost $3.10

HANDS-ON 15 MIN.   TOTAL 15 MIN.   SERVES 4

This slaw is a stunner. It's fantastically crunchy, sweet, tart, and just the right amount of sharp. It'll pair well with all kinds of roasted and grilled meats and most Latin-inspired flavors. It's also perfect as a side for a sandwich. It's just so fresh and healthy. Make the jam ahead so you can quickly throw this slaw together. When fresh strawberries go out of season, use your favorite flavor of prepared jam for a different twist on this versatile slaw. Use a mix of red, yellow, or orange bell peppers if you like or have them on hand.

1 ½ cups thinly sliced jicama

¼ cup thinly sliced red onion

¼ cup fresh mint leaves

1 red bell pepper, thinly sliced

½ teaspoon salt

⅛ teaspoon freshly ground black pepper

Pinch of ground cayenne pepper

3 tablespoons Strawberry-Lemonade Jam (page 217)

2 tablespoons olive oil

4 ½ teaspoons fresh lemon juice

Toss together the jicama, onion, mint leaves, and bell pepper in a large bowl. Sprinkle with the salt and peppers. Whisk together the jam, olive oil, and lemon juice. Drizzle over the salad; toss to coat.

Jicama

Jicama is a juicy root veggie with a marvelously crisp texture that doesn't get soggy when tossed into a salad, salsa, or slaw. Because of the mild, neutral flavor, it's one of the most versatile veggies around. It's native to Mexico and used often in Latin cooking, so look for this vegetable in the produce section at your Hispanic market.

Homemade Guacamole & Chips

Peel and seed 1 ripe avocado. Place the avocado in a mixing bowl; toss with 2 teaspoons fresh lemon juice. Mash the avocado to the desired consistency. Stir in 2 tablespoons minced onion, 2 tablespoons chopped plum tomato, $1/8$ to $1/4$ teaspoon garlic powder, and a pinch of ground cayenne pepper. Season to taste. Serve with $1/2$ (11-ounce) bag of tortilla chips. (Pictured on page 148.)

Spinach & Herb Salad with Strawberry Vinaigrette

Whisk together 2 tablespoons extra-virgin olive oil, $1 1/2$ tablespoons cider vinegar, and 1 tablespoon water into 2 tablespoons Strawberry Lemonade Jam (page 217). Stir in $1/2$ teaspoon sugar, $1/2$ teaspoon minced fresh garlic, $1/4$ teaspoon kosher salt, $1/4$ teaspoon Dijon mustard, and $1/8$ teaspoon freshly ground black pepper. Toss dressing with 6 cups baby spinach, $1/4$ cup coarsely chopped fresh basil, and $1/4$ cup finely sliced red onion. Season to taste with salt and freshly ground black pepper.

Caesar Salad with Garlicky Croutons & Homemade Dressing

Toss 1 cup torn crusty bread with 1 tablespoon melted butter, 1 tablespoon extra-virgin olive oil, and $1/4$ teaspoon garlic powder; spread in a single layer on a baking sheet. Sprinkle with salt, and bake at 400°F for 8 minutes or until crisp. Cool to room temperature. Meanwhile, stir 2 tablespoons extra-virgin olive oil, 1 tablespoon grated Parmesan cheese, 1 teaspoon anchovy paste, and $1/4$ teaspoon finely minced fresh garlic into $1/4$ cup Alabama-Style White BBQ Sauce (page 222) or mayonnaise. Toss 4 cups torn romaine and $1/4$ cup thinly sliced red onion with the croutons and dressing.

Summer Salad

Toss 1 sliced small ripe peach, $1/2$ cup sliced tomato, and 2 paper-thin slices red onion with 2 tablespoons Lemon Vinaigrette (page 213). Add 1 cup arugula, and season to taste with salt and pepper. Toss gently. (Pictured on page 93.)

Caramelized Pineapple & Avocado Salad

Arrange the top rack of the oven 5 inches from the broiler element. Preheat the broiler to high. Line a broiler-safe baking sheet with foil, and coat with cooking spray. Whisk 1 tablespoon extra-virgin olive oil into 2 tablespoons brown sugar. Peel and slice half of a ripe pineapple into $1/2$-inch-thick rings. Remove the core from the pineapple rings, and place rings in a single layer on prepared baking sheet. Brush half of the sugar mixture over 1 side of the pineapple rings; sprinkle with $1/8$ teaspoon kosher salt. Broil for 2 minutes or until golden. Turn the pineapple rings over; brush with the remaining half of the sugar mixture. Broil for 2 minutes or until golden. Let the pineapple stand at room temperature for 5 minutes; chop. Meanwhile, peel, pit, and chop 1 medium-sized ripe avocado, and place in a medium mixing bowl. Toss the avocado with $1 1/2$ tablespoons fresh lime juice. Finely chop 2 tablespoons red onion and 1 tablespoon fresh mint leaves; add to the bowl with the avocado. Stir in the chopped pineapple, $1/8$ teaspoon kosher salt, $1/8$ teaspoon ground cumin, and $1/8$ teaspoon ground cayenne pepper; toss. (Pictured on page 162.)

Total Cost $1.69
Cucumber Salad

Trim and chop 1 English cucumber. Toss with ½ teaspoon dark sesame oil. Add the zest and juice of 1 lime to the bowl with the cucumber; toss. Season to taste with salt and pepper. Sprinkle 2 tablespoons chopped fresh chives over the top. (Pictured on page 106.)

Total Cost $4.15
Asparagus with Pickled Red Onion

Thinly vertically slice 1 medium-sized red onion, and place in a large metal bowl. Bring ½ cup water, ½ cup sugar, ¼ cup red wine vinegar, 2 tablespoons kosher salt, 1 teaspoon whole black peppercorns, ⅛ teaspoon crushed red pepper, 1 bay leaf, and 1 smashed garlic clove to a boil. Cook until the sugar and salt dissolve. Immediately strain the boiling liquid through a sieve over the onions in the bowl; cover tightly with plastic wrap. Let the mixture stand until cool and onions are crisp-tender; strain. Chill until ready to serve. Serve over 1 pound trimmed, steamed asparagus.

Total Cost $2.90
Roasted Brussels Sprouts

Cook 1 bacon slice in a small skillet over medium heat until crisp. Remove the bacon from the pan, reserving the drippings. Crumble the bacon, and set aside. Trim and halve 1 pound of fresh Brussels sprouts; toss with the reserved bacon drippings, 2 tablespoons melted butter, and 1 tablespoon honey. Sprinkle with ½ teaspoon kosher salt and ¼ teaspoon freshly ground black pepper. Roast the sprouts mixture at 400°F for 15 to 20 minutes or until the sprouts are golden. Sprinkle with the bacon. (Pictured on page 102.)

Total Cost $1.44
Roasted Green Beans with Browned Butter

Trim 1 pound fresh green beans; toss with 1 tablespoon canola oil. Roast at 425°F for 8 minutes or until crisp-tender. Place the beans on a serving platter. Add 3 tablespoons butter to the roasting pan, and place it back in the oven for 2 to 3 minutes or until the butter melts and browns. Drizzle the butter over the beans; season to taste with salt and pepper.

Winter Roots

- **Carrots:** Add interest to your veggie cooking with multicolor carrots. At $2.50 per bag, you'll want to reserve these for special occasions. Buy just one bag and mix them with regular orange carrots to stretch your dollar.

- **Parsnips:** Think of these as carrots, only sweeter and a bit earthier at the same time.

- **Radishes:** These pungent roots come in lots of shapes and sizes. Look for pastel colors, called Easter radishes, in the spring. If you see watermelon radishes, with a green exterior, thin white "rind" layer, and bright pink/red middle, give them a try as well.

- **Turnips:** Try mixing turnips with potatoes for a less-starchy, lower-calorie side.

- **Rutabaga:** If turnips have too much bite, try rutabagas, turnips' milder-flavored cousins.

- **Beets:** Look for golden beets at farmers' markets, Whole Foods, and sometimes in the supermarket. They're easier to work with since they won't stain, and the mild flavor is a welcome change for those who find red beets too earthy. You may also stumble across candy-cane beets, with a red-and-white striped center.

- **Celery root:** This knobby root has a mild celery-like flavor. Slice or chop it and serve it raw in salads or slaws. You can also roast it for a side or simmer it in soups and stews.

Total Cost $1.08

Roasted Broccoli

HANDS-ON: 5 MIN. TOTAL 15 MIN. SERVES 4

Roasting broccoli brings out the earthy flavor and makes a nice basic side that's super versatile. When you have a couple of bucks to spare in your dinner budget, jazz up the broccoli with one of my flavorful finishes below and at right.

6 cups chopped broccoli florets

1 tablespoon canola oil

Kosher salt and freshly ground black pepper

2 teaspoons olive oil

1. Preheat the oven to 450°F.

2. Place the broccoli on a rimmed baking sheet; drizzle with the canola oil. Sprinkle the broccoli with salt and pepper. Roast at 450°F for 8 to 10 minutes or until slightly charred but still crisp-tender. Remove the pan from the oven. Drizzle the warm broccoli with the olive oil; toss. Season to taste with salt and pepper.

Total Cost: $1.50

Garlic-Chile Roasted Broccoli

Follow the recipe as directed, omitting the olive oil. While the broccoli cooks, combine 2 teaspoons toasted sesame oil, 1/2 teaspoon minced fresh garlic, 1/2 teaspoon sambal oelek (ground fresh chile paste), 1/8 teaspoon kosher salt, 1/8 teaspoon ground cumin, and 1/8 teaspoon ground coriander; toss with the hot cooked broccoli.

Total Cost $1.99

Lemony-Parm Roasted Broccoli

Follow the recipe as directed, adding 1/2 teaspoon grated fresh lemon zest, 2 teaspoons fresh lemon juice, and 1 ounce shredded Parmesan cheese to the broccoli when adding the olive oil.

Total Cost $2.08

Walnut-Thyme Roasted Broccoli

Follow the recipe as directed, omitting the olive oil. Instead, drizzle the broccoli with 2 teaspoons toasted walnut oil. Sprinkle the broccoli mixture with 2 tablespoons chopped toasted walnuts and 1 teaspoon chopped fresh thyme leaves; toss.

Total Cost $1.68

Anchovy-Basil Butter Roasted Broccoli

Follow the recipe as directed, omitting the olive oil. While the broccoli cooks, combine 1 1/2 tablespoons softened butter, 2 teaspoons chopped fresh basil, 3/4 teaspoon finely chopped shallot, and 1/2 teaspoon anchovy paste; toss with the hot cooked broccoli.

Total Cost: $2.10

Sicilian-Style Roasted Broccoli

Follow the recipe as directed. Add 3 tablespoons dried cherries, 2 tablespoons chopped pitted kalamata olives, and 1/2 teaspoon grated fresh orange zest; toss. Sprinkle with 2 tablespoons crumbled goat cheese.

Lemony-Parm
Roasted Broccoli

Home Fries

HANDS-ON **42 MIN.**   TOTAL **1 HR., 10 MIN.**   SERVES **4**

Home fries are the ultimate comfort-food side. They brown beautifully and have a rich flavor that both your grown-up and kid friends will love. Briefly microwaving the potatoes gives them a head start on cooking. Quick tip: Adding butter not only helps them brown better, but also lends rich flavor. Waxy potatoes won't break down in the pan when cubed and sautéed.

1 pound Yukon Gold or red-skinned potatoes, scrubbed and cubed

2 tablespoons canola oil, divided

1 1/2 cups chopped yellow onion

4 garlic cloves, minced

2 tablespoons butter

1/2 teaspoon kosher salt

1/2 teaspoon freshly ground black pepper

1 tablespoon coarsely chopped fresh flat-leaf parsley

1. Place the potatoes in a microwave-safe dish, and cover with plastic wrap. Microwave at HIGH for 5 minutes. Uncover and cool slightly.

2. Heat a large skillet over medium heat. Add 1 tablespoon oil to the pan; swirl to coat. Add the onion; cook 20 minutes or until golden and tender, stirring occasionally. Add the garlic; cook 1 minute, stirring constantly. Remove the onion mixture from the pan.

3. Increase the heat to medium-high. Add the remaining 1 tablespoon oil and the butter to the pan, and swirl to coat. Add the potatoes, and cook 4 minutes, without stirring. Turn the potatoes over. Cook 6 minutes or until browned, without stirring. Reduce the heat to medium-low; cook 10 minutes or until tender and golden brown, stirring occasionally. Remove from the heat. Stir in the onion mixture, salt, and pepper; toss. Sprinkle with the parsley.

Total cost $2.07

Potato Smashers

HANDS-ON **20 MIN.**   TOTAL **50 MIN.**   SERVES **4**

Total cost
$2.49

I promise your whole family and everyone you know will become addicted to these wonderfully delicious potatoes. Since the strength of heat varies so much from one stovetop to the next, start checking your potatoes for doneness after they've boiled for 5 minutes. Your potatoes may cook a good bit faster or slower than mine do on my electric stovetop.

12 ounces red-skinned potatoes, scrubbed and cut into 1-inch chunks

6 tablespoons bacon drippings

1 ½ teaspoons kosher salt

¼ teaspoon freshly ground black pepper

2 tablespoons unsalted butter, softened

1 tablespoon chopped fresh flat-leaf parsley

1 teaspoon minced shallot

1 teaspoon minced fresh garlic

1 teaspoon minced fresh thyme

1. Place the potatoes in a saucepan; cover to 2 inches above the potatoes with cold water. Bring the potatoes to a boil over medium-high heat. Boil the potatoes for 8 to 10 minutes or until the potatoes are fork-tender. Drain.

2. Meanwhile, place a small shallow roasting pan in the oven. Preheat the oven and pan to 450°F.

3. Carefully remove the hot pan from the oven. Melt the bacon drippings in the hot pan; swirl to coat. Carefully arrange the cooked potatoes in a single layer in the hot pan; sprinkle with the salt and pepper. Mash the potatoes flat with a potato masher or spatula. Bake the potatoes at 450°F for 20 to 22 minutes or until the potatoes are crisp and golden on the outside and tender in the center.

4. While the potatoes bake, mash together the butter, parsley, shallot, garlic, and thyme. Add the butter mixture to the hot potato mixture; toss to coat. Season to taste with salt and pepper.

Total Cost $1.08

Sweet Potato Wedges

Peel 1 1/4 pounds sweet potatoes, and cut into wedges; toss with 2 tablespoons canola oil. Sprinkle with 1 teaspoon kosher salt, 1/4 teaspoon sugar, 1/4 teaspoon ground cumin, 1/8 teaspoon garlic powder, 1/8 teaspoon ground cinnamon, and freshly ground black pepper; toss. Roast at 425°F for 18 minutes. Stir and roast for 5 to 10 more minutes or until the potatoes are golden and tender. Sprinkle with 1 teaspoon chopped fresh sage.

Total Cost $3.29

Pineapple Tossed with Coconut

Halve a fresh pineapple; reserve one half for another use. Peel remaining pineapple half, core, and chop. Place in a bowl. Add 1/3 cup unsweetened toasted coconut flakes, 1 tablespoon brown sugar, and 1 tablespoon fresh lime juice. Sprinkle fruit with a pinch of salt; toss.

Total Cost $2.19

Chickpea & Tomato Toss

Combine 1/2 cup Marinated Tomatoes (page 209) and 1 1/2 cups Roasted Chickpeas (page 206); toss. Season to taste with salt and pepper.

Total Cost $1.45

Pea Soup

Melt 1 tablespoon bacon drippings and 1 tablespoon butter in a saucepan over medium-low heat. Add 1 cup finely chopped yellow onion to the pan; cook 8 minutes or until the onion is almost soft. Stir in 2 teaspoons minced fresh garlic paste; cook 2 minutes. Stir in 1 (8-ounce) bag frozen English peas, 2 1/2 cups Overnight Chicken Stock (page 218), 1 teaspoon kosher salt, and 1/2 teaspoon freshly ground black pepper. Increase the heat to medium-high; bring to a boil. Reduce the heat to medium, cover, and cook for 15 to 20 minutes. Remove from the heat; let stand 5 minutes. Scrape the mixture into a blender; process until smooth. Stir in enough heavy cream, about 1/4 cup, to reach the desired consistency. Season to taste with salt and pepper. (Pictured on page 113.)

Total Cost $3.80

Blistered Tomatoes & Baguette

Toss 1 pint red cherry tomatoes with 3 whole garlic cloves, 1 tablespoon olive oil, and 1 teaspoon kosher salt; roast at 425°F for 12 to 15 minutes. Drizzle the mixture with 2 teaspoons balsamic vinegar and 1 teaspoon fresh lemon juice. Crumble 1/4 cup feta cheese over the top. Roast for 5 more minutes or until the tomatoes are charred. Remove the garlic; pound and chop it. Toss with the tomato mixture. Serve warm with an 8-ounce sliced French bread baguette.

Total Cost $0.64

Garlicky Toast

Preheat the broiler to low. Melt 2 tablespoons butter in the microwave. Stir 1 teaspoon minced fresh garlic paste into the butter. Halve 2 slices of sourdough bread diagonally to form 4 bread triangles. Arrange the bread in a single layer on a baking sheet; broil 2 minutes or until toasted. Turn the bread over; brush with the garlic butter, and sprinkle with salt. Broil for 1 to 2 minutes or just until toasted, taking care not to burn the garlic.

Total Cost $1.27

Cauliflower Rice

Preheat the broiler to high. Line a rimmed baking sheet with aluminum foil. Brush 1 tablespoon canola oil over the aluminum, and spread 6 cups coarsely shredded cauliflower in an even layer over the prepared pan. Broil the cauliflower on high for 10 to 15 minutes, or until golden brown, rotating the pan after 6 minutes (I used the top rack in the oven). Melt 2 1/2 tablespoons butter in a small saucepan over medium heat. Add 3/4 teaspoon minced fresh garlic to the pan; cook 1 minute or just until fragrant (do not brown). Remove from the heat. Scrape the roasted cauliflower into a serving bowl; drizzle with the garlic butter. Sprinkle with 1/2 teaspoon kosher salt and 1/4 teaspoon freshly ground black pepper; toss to combine.

Total Cost $2.18

Sesame Rice

Toss 2 cups hot cooked rice with 1 tablespoon toasted sesame oil and 1 teaspoon sesame seeds. Season to taste with salt and pepper. Toss 1 peeled chopped small avocado with the juice of 1 lime. Add to the rice; stir gently. (Pictured on page 88.)

Total Cost $0.75

Browned Butter Rice Pilaf

Melt 1/4 cup butter in a small saucepan over medium-high heat. Cook the butter until bubbly and golden brown. Skim the top, and toss the browned butter with 2 cups hot cooked rice. Season to taste with salt and pepper. (Pictured on page 117.)

Total Cost $2.00

Slow-Cooker Grits

Stir together 2 cups uncooked stone-ground grits, 1/2 cup melted butter, and 1 tablespoon kosher salt in a 5-quart slow cooker; stir in 6 cups water. Cover and cook on LOW 8 hours. Stir just before serving. Makes about 8 cups.

Total Cost $2.14

Parmesan-Pepper Polenta

Bring 1 1/2 cups whole milk and 1/2 cup Overnight Chicken Stock (page 218) to a boil in a medium saucepan over medium-high heat. Reduce heat to medium. Stir in 1/2 cup polenta or stone-ground yellow grits, 1 teaspoon kosher salt, 1 teaspoon minced fresh garlic, and 1/2 teaspoon black pepper; cook, stirring frequently, until liquid is absorbed, about 20 minutes. Remove from heat. Add 4 ounces softened cream cheese and 1/4 cup grated Parmesan cheese to the hot polenta; stir until the cheeses melt and are thoroughly blended into the polenta. Adjust the seasoning as needed, and serve immediately.

PANTRY BASICS

After investing your energies and efforts budgeting and bargain shopping, the last thing you want to do is spend any of your hard-earned savings on last-minute dashes to the supermarket just to get dinner on the table. Because those are usually the most costly. So plan ahead, stock your larder, and keep a few tasty DIY sauces and condiments on hand to keep your grocery budget in check.

Roasted Chickpeas

HANDS-ON **15 MIN.** TOTAL **27 MIN.** MAKES **2 ½ CUPS**

Total cost
$2.42

This is a wonderful recipe for all sorts of uses. I use it as a soup topper—it's especially delicious with Smoky Tomato Soup (page 167). It'll add flavor, texture, and hearty goodness to salads. Or, roast them a bit longer, until the chickpeas become crunchy, and it's a delicious snack.

1 ½ tablespoons minced shallots

5 garlic cloves, coarsely chopped

1 cup chopped country ham

1 (15.5-ounce) can chickpeas, drained and rinsed

1 tablespoon extra-virgin olive oil

1 ½ teaspoons kosher salt

¼ teaspoon ground cumin

1. Preheat the oven to 450°F.

2. Combine the first 4 ingredients in a mixing bowl. Drizzle with the oil; toss with the salt and cumin. Spread the mixture in a single layer in a small roasting pan. Roast at 450°F for 12 minutes, stirring once.

Have a Little Fun with Your Favorite Flavors.

• **Maple & Bacon Chickpeas:** Substitute 2 to 3 slices chopped smoked bacon for the ham and omit the cumin. Toss with 2 teaspoons maple syrup before roasting.

• **Smoke & Spice Chickpeas:** Prepare the recipe, adding ½ teaspoon smoked paprika and ¼ teaspoon crushed red pepper before roasting.

• **Wasabi & Sesame Chickpeas:** Prepare the recipe, adding 1 ½ teaspoons wasabi powder, 1 teaspoon dark sesame oil, and ½ teaspoon sesame seeds before roasting. Toss with ½ teaspoon grated fresh lemon zest and more wasabi powder, if desired, after roasting, while chickpeas are still hot.

Marinated Tomatoes

Total cost
$1.95

HANDS-ON 10 MIN.   TOTAL 30 MIN.   MAKES ABOUT 1 CUP

These tomatoes are lovely. Nicely seasoned, flavored with garlic, lemon, and thyme, and bathed in fruity olive oil. It's just the right topping for grilled chicken, fish, pork, or beef. Or spoon them over a salad since the tomato juices marry with the olive oil to make a faux vinaigrette.

1 cup quartered cherry tomatoes

1 1/2 teaspoons finely minced fresh shallots

3/4 teaspoon minced fresh garlic

1/2 teaspoon finely chopped fresh thyme leaves

1/4 teaspoon kosher salt

1/4 teaspoon grated fresh lemon zest

1/8 teaspoon freshly ground black pepper

1 1/2 tablespoons extra-virgin olive oil

Combine the tomatoes, shallots, garlic, thyme, salt, lemon zest, and pepper in a small bowl; toss. Drizzle the oil over the tomato mixture; toss. Let stand for 20 minutes.

TIGHTWAD TIP
Buying Tomatoes

Last summer, I found the best price on red grape tomatoes for everyday use at Trader Joe's. When I'm looking to impress—and I have an extra dollar or two—I'll splurge on the multicolored tomatoes, which work beautifully in this recipe too.

Lemon Ricotta

HANDS-ON **15 MIN.**   TOTAL **5 HR., 15 MIN.**   MAKES **ABOUT 1²/₃ CUPS**

Total cost
$3.28

Think you don't like ricotta because of the grainy texture in store-bought versions? All it takes is one taste of this delicious creamy version to make you a convert. Dollop it on pizza or pasta for a lovely finishing touch.

4 cups whole milk

1 cup half-and-half

¹/₂ cup whole-milk buttermilk

¹/₂ cup plain whole-milk Greek yogurt

Cheesecloth

**Grated fresh lemon zest from
    1 medium lemon**

1 tablespoon extra-virgin olive oil

1 teaspoon kosher salt

1. Whisk together the first 4 ingredients in a medium saucepan over medium heat; bring just to a boil. Remove from the heat; let stand for 3 minutes, stirring occasionally. Strain the mixture through a sieve lined with 2 layers of cheesecloth. (Do not wring out moisture.)

2. Scrape the hot ricotta into a small bowl; stir in the lemon zest and remaining ingredients. Cool to room temperature. Cover and chill for 4 hours or until ready to use.

3 Ways with Lemon Ricotta

• For a quick dessert or snack, spoon the ricotta into a bowl and top with granola or fresh fruit. Then drizzle with honey, if you like.

• Jazz up your breakfast by adding a schmear of Lemon Ricotta to your avocado toast or scrambled eggs.

• Brown breakfast sausage with onion and garlic. Stir into Lemon Ricotta and use as a filling for pasta shells.

Lemon Vinaigrette

Total cost $1.37

HANDS-ON 15 MIN.   TOTAL 15 MIN.   MAKES ABOUT ⅔ CUP

Here's a tangy-sweet dressing that brightens any salad greens, but why stop there? You can toss it with cooked whole grains and roasted or grilled veggies for lively side dishes. It's also a quick and inexpensive way to boost the flavor of grilled chicken, shrimp, or fish. Depending how you plan to use it, you can also add your favorite chopped fresh herbs to make the vinaigrette that much better.

1 teaspoon freshly grated lemon zest

⅓ cup fresh lemon juice (about 2 small lemons)

1 tablespoon honey

2 teaspoons sugar

1 teaspoon Dijon mustard

¼ cup extra-virgin olive oil

1 tablespoon canola oil

2 teaspoons minced shallot

¼ teaspoon kosher salt

⅛ teaspoon freshly ground black pepper

Microplane Zester

If you had just one gadget in your kitchen, it should be this one. Remember to grate just the yellow zest and stop when you get down to the white pith. And always zest before you juice.

Combine the first 5 ingredients in a small mixing bowl, whisking until blended. Drizzle the olive oil in a slow, steady stream into the bowl with the lemon mixture, whisking constantly and vigorously to incorporate the oil into the mixture. Once the olive oil is incorporated, repeat the procedure with the canola oil. Whisk in the shallot and remaining ingredients. Adjust seasoning as needed.

TIGHTWAD TIP Storing Vinaigrette

If you don't use the vinaigrette all at once, just cover and keep the rest refrigerated for up to two weeks. After it's been chilled, be sure to shake or stir vigorously before using.

Avocado-Ranch Dressing

Total cost
$1.75
per quart

HANDS-ON 10 MIN.   TOTAL 10 MIN.   MAKES 1¼ CUPS

This dressing is great drizzled over salads or served with basic grilled or roasted meats and seafood. It's a fantastic sauce for crab cakes, and it makes a tasty dip for crunchy veggies too. Though I normally use parsley to make it, I prefer cilantro when I want to serve it with Latin-inspired foods. Use whichever you prefer.

½ medium avocado, peeled, pitted, and chopped

2 tablespoons fresh lime juice

⅓ cup whole buttermilk

2 tablespoons chopped fresh flat-leaf parsley or cilantro leaves

2 tablespoons Mexican crema or sour cream

¾ teaspoon kosher salt

¾ teaspoon minced fresh garlic

1 green onion, trimmed

Pinch of ground cayenne pepper

2 tablespoons canola oil

Toss the avocado with lime juice. Place the avocado mixture in a blender with the buttermilk, parsley, crema, kosher salt, garlic, green onion, and cayenne pepper; process until smooth. Add the canola oil; process to combine. Cover and chill until ready to serve.

Strawberry Lemonade Jam

Total cost
$2.39
per quart

HANDS-ON **20 MIN.**   TOTAL **2 HR., 20 MIN.**   MAKES **ABOUT 1 ²/₃ CUPS**

Use this delightful homemade jam in all the ways you might use any other. Spread some on your morning toast or bagel, or use it for filling between the layers of a cake, for example. It's also useful in savory applications as well: Try it as the base for a fantastic sweet-tart Strawberry Vinaigrette (page 194), or use it to dress Jicama & Bell Pepper Slaw (page 193).

2 ½ cups coarsely chopped fresh strawberries

¾ cup sugar

¼ cup fresh lemon juice

3 tablespoons cornstarch

1. Place the strawberries in a blender; process until smooth. Press strawberry mixture through a mesh strainer into a 3-quart saucepan, using the back of a spoon to squeeze out the juice; discard the pulp. Stir in the sugar.

2. Whisk together the lemon juice and cornstarch; gradually whisk the lemon juice mixture into the strawberry mixture. Bring the mixture to a boil over medium heat, and cook, whisking constantly, for 1 minute. Remove from the heat. Place plastic wrap directly on the warm jam; chill 2 hours or until cold. Refrigerate in an airtight container.

TIGHTWAD TIP
Stock Up in Season

Make a mega batch of this jam in the spring when berries are in season, plentiful, and most affordable. Then spoon the jam into canning jars, and seal them to extend the life.

Overnight Chicken Stock

Total cost
$0.10
per quart

HANDS-ON 35 MIN. TOTAL 9 HR., 5 MIN. MAKES ABOUT 6 QUARTS

Chicken stock is every great cook's secret weapon. It adds immeasurable flavor to so many dishes. Buying prepared stock or broth from the grocery store is one of the worst ways to spend your valuable grocery dollars. Why? Because if you make your own, it'll taste *SO* much better, and you can make it for mere pennies. In fact, it's best if you use remnants that would have otherwise gone unused, such as chicken bones, onion and carrot peels, and celery ends. If you get in the habit of saving these instead of tossing them out and putting on a batch of stock to simmer slowly all day or overnight in a low oven, it's a breeze to make your own.

2 whole chicken carcasses

6 cups onion peels and trimmings or 1 large onion with peel, cut into wedges

2 cups carrot peels and trimmings or 2 medium carrots with tops and peels, cut into 1-inch pieces

1 tablespoon whole black peppercorns

2 bay leaves

Stems from 1 bunch fresh flat-leaf parsley

Bottom and trimmings from 1 bunch celery or 2 ribs, cut into 1-inch pieces

2 gallons cold water

Cheesecloth

1. Preheat the oven to 225°F.

2. Place the first 7 ingredients in a stockpot. Pour 2 gallons cold water over the top. Bring just to a boil over medium heat, skimming any foam or particles that rise to the surface.

3. Place the pot in the oven, and bake, uncovered, at 225°F for at least 8 hours or until the stock is golden. Cool at room temperature for 30 minutes. Strain the stock through a cheesecloth-lined sieve; discard the solids. Cool stock completely. Cover and keep in the fridge for 1 week, or freeze for up to 3 months.

All-Purpose Tomato Sauce

Total cost $2.88

HANDS-ON **15 MIN.**   TOTAL **4 HR.**   MAKES **5 ½ CUPS**

Anchovy paste normally comes in a small tube and should be available at your local supermarket or in the grocery department of big-box stores. It usually lives on the pasta aisle near jarred sauces and Italian-style condiments, but it's sometimes found with canned fish. This potent ingredient is pretty affordable and worth seeking out. See the tip below for more suggested uses.

¼ cup extra-virgin olive oil

2 cups chopped yellow onion

8 large garlic cloves, peeled and smashed

2 tablespoons tomato paste

2 tablespoons red wine vinegar

2 teaspoons kosher salt

2 teaspoons anchovy paste

¼ teaspoon crushed red pepper

2 (28-ounce) cans crushed tomatoes

1 Parmesan cheese rind

Pinch of sugar

1. Preheat the oven to 300°F.

2. Heat a large oven-safe cast-iron or other heavy 12-inch skillet over medium-high heat. Add the oil to the pan; swirl to coat. Stir in the onion, and sauté for 2 to 3 minutes or until the onion just begins to soften, stirring frequently. Do not brown. Add the garlic; sauté for 1 minute, stirring constantly. Stir in the tomato paste; cook for 30 seconds, smearing the tomato paste over the bottom of the pan to "fry" it a little.

3. Stir in the vinegar and remaining ingredients; bring to a boil, stirring to combine. Place the skillet in the oven, and bake, uncovered, at 300°F for 2½ hours or until the sauce has charred slightly around the edges and concentrated in thickness and flavor, stirring after the first 1½ hours. Cool for 30 minutes. Process the sauce in a blender or food processor until smooth. Cool completely. Cover and refrigerate, or freeze until ready to use.

🪙 TIGHTWAD TIP Use It, Don't Lose It: Anchovy Paste

Anchovy paste takes the best of this salty little fish and makes it better by processing it with a little oil, vinegar, salt, and a pinch of sugar to make a smooth savory paste. Don't worry, it doesn't taste fishy, just meaty and rich. Use just a dab to round out the flavor of all kinds of dishes. I use anchovy paste in two recipes in this book: All-Purpose Tomato Sauce and to make

Caesar salad dressing on page 194. Here are even more ways to use the rest of the tube:

- Use a bit in marinades for beef and pork.
- Add depth to soups and stews.
- Mix it with mayo, sour cream, and a squeeze of lemon juice to make dressing for potato salad.

- Make a rich, meaty sauce for pasta by combining pasta water and anchovy paste. Finish with a bit of butter or Parmesan cheese.
- Whisk together olive oil, garlic, anchovy paste, and herbs to brush over pizza crust.

Alabama-Style White BBQ Sauce

Total cost $1.19

HANDS-ON **18 MIN.**   TOTAL **18 MIN.**   MAKES **1 ¹/₂ CUPS**

I had never heard of white BBQ sauce before I moved to Birmingham. It's a completely addictive northern Alabama creation. You'll want to keep a jar in your fridge at all times! It's delicious served as a sauce for chicken fingers and equally good with veggies for dipping. It also works as a tasty sandwich spread. I use it in place of red sauce on pizzas (White Chicken Pizza, page 31) and to moisten meatloaf (Turkey-Bacon-Cheddar Meatloaf, page 78). Once you try it, I know you'll find countless ways to enjoy it.

1 whole lemon

6 tablespoons distilled white vinegar

³/₄ teaspoon kosher salt

¹/₂ teaspoon minced fresh garlic

¹/₄ teaspoon freshly ground black pepper

1 cup mayonnaise

1. Use a veggie peeler to cut away 2 (1-inch) strips zest from the lemon, taking care to shave off just the bright yellow zest, and leaving all the bitter white pith behind on the fruit. Place the zest in blender jar. Once you shave off the zest strips, slice off just enough of both ends of the lemon to see the pulp. Stand the lemon up on one end, and run your knife between the visible white pith and the pulp to peel half of the fruit. Halve the lemon, reserving the half with the peel for another use. Cut the peeled half in half, reserving half for another use. Place the remaining peeled lemon quarter in the blender with the zest.

2. Add the vinegar and remaining ingredients to the blender; process until smooth, scraping the sides as needed. Cover and chill up to 2 weeks.

Bacon & Chive Breadcrumbs

Total cost $1.28

HANDS-ON 15 MIN.   TOTAL 15 MIN.   MAKES ABOUT 1 CUP

A perfect use for day-old baguette, the tasty breadcrumbs are great sprinkled atop salads and pasta or tossed with roasted veggies. If you have any left over, keep them in a small plastic ziplock bag. To preserve their freshness, press all the excess air out of the bag before you seal it.

2 slices applewood-smoked bacon

3 ounces torn baguette

3 tablespoons unsalted butter

$1/4$ teaspoon kosher salt

1 tablespoon chopped fresh chives

TIGHTWAD TIP
Save That Stale Bread

Don't toss out old bread. Bag and store it in the freezer, so you can make tasty breadcrumbs, bread pudding, bread salad, croutons, and all sorts of yumminess on the cheap.

1. Cook the bacon in a medium sauté pan over medium heat until crisp. Remove the bacon from the pan; drain the bacon on paper towels. Reserve 2 teaspoons bacon drippings in the pan; set aside any remaining bacon drippings for another use. Crumble the bacon.

2. Pulse the baguette in a food processor until coarse crumbs form. Heat the pan with the drippings over medium-high heat. Add the butter, swirling to melt. Add the breadcrumbs and salt; sauté for 2 minutes or until golden, stirring frequently. Remove from the heat; stir in the crumbled bacon and chives.

Total Cost: $1.02

Parsley & Parmesan Breadcrumbs

Prepare Bacon & Chive Breadcrumbs as directed, omitting the bacon and chives. Stir in 3 tablespoons grated Parmesan cheese and 1 tablespoon chopped fresh parsley.

Grissini

HANDS-ON **30 MIN.**   TOTAL **2 HR.**   MAKES **20 BREADSTICKS**

Terrific for a party snack or a side, these small crisp Italian-style breadsticks are absolutely addictive, and they're easy to make. Enjoy any extras with hummus or your favorite dip.

Total cost $2.37

$1/2$ cup warm water (100° to 110°F)

$1/2$ ($1/4$-ounce) package active dry yeast ($1 \frac{1}{8}$ teaspoons)

1 teaspoon sugar

$1 \frac{1}{2}$ tablespoons extra-virgin olive oil

$1/4$ cup grated Parmesan cheese, divided

$1/2$ teaspoon kosher salt

$1 \frac{1}{2}$ cups plus 2 tablespoons all-purpose flour (about 6.18 ounces)

Cooking spray

1 tablespoon canola oil

1 tablespoon butter

$1/2$ teaspoon minced fresh garlic

1. Combine $1/2$ cup warm water, yeast, and sugar in the bowl of a stand mixer with the paddle attachment; let stand for 5 minutes or until bubbly. Add the olive oil, 2 tablespoons cheese, and salt to the yeast mixture; beat to combine. Weigh or lightly spoon flour into dry measuring cups; level with a knife. With the mixer on medium-low speed, gradually add the flour into the bowl; beat to combine. Turn the dough out onto a floured surface, and knead 8 to 10 times or until a soft elastic dough forms. Place the dough in a large bowl coated with cooking spray, turning to coat the top. Cover the dough with plastic wrap; let stand in a warm place (85°F), free from drafts, for 1 hour or until doubled in size. Punch the dough down.

2. Preheat the oven to 425°F.

3. Turn the dough out onto a lightly floured surface. Roll the dough into an 8- x 6-inch rectangle. Brush the dough evenly with the canola oil; sprinkle evenly with the remaining 2 tablespoons cheese. Cut the dough lengthwise into 20 thin strips using a pizza cutter. Place the strips on a baking sheet coated with cooking spray. Bake in batches at 425°F for 8 to 12 minutes or until golden and crisp.

4. Melt the butter. Add the garlic to the butter, stirring to distribute. Brush over the grissini.

Feta & Red Onion Focaccia

Total cost $2.81

HANDS-ON 30 MIN.   TOTAL 2 HR., 30 MIN.   MAKES 1 (9-INCH) SQUARE LOAF

Use the lovely, puffy bread to make sandwiches, or cut it into smaller squares for an appetizer platter. If you have leftovers, wrap tightly with plastic wrap and freeze for later. Or cut it into cubes, toss with a bit of olive oil, and toast them to create croutons.

¾ cup warm water (100° to 110°F)

1 (¼-ounce) package rapid-rise yeast (2 ¼ teaspoons)

1 teaspoon sugar

½ cup extra-virgin olive oil, divided

1 teaspoon minced fresh garlic

1 ¼ teaspoons kosher salt

2 ¼ cups all-purpose flour (about 10.13 ounces)

Cooking spray

½ cup crumbled feta cheese

⅓ cup vertically sliced red onion

1. Combine ¾ cup warm water, yeast, and sugar in the bowl of a stand mixer with the paddle attachment; let stand for 5 minutes or until bubbly. Add ¼ cup oil, garlic, and salt to the yeast mixture; beat to combine. Weigh or lightly spoon flour into dry measuring cups; level with a knife. With the mixer on low speed, gradually sprinkle the flour into the bowl; beat until a sticky dough forms. Turn the dough out onto a floured surface, and knead until the dough is smooth and elastic. Place the dough in a large bowl coated with cooking spray, turning to coat the top. Cover the dough with plastic wrap; let stand in a warm place (85°F), free from drafts, for 1 hour or until doubled in size.

2. Preheat the oven to 400°F. Brush a 9-inch square pan with 2 tablespoons of the oil.

3. Gently stretch the dough into the prepared pan; press your fingers into the top of the dough to leave indentations. Carefully place the crumbled feta in the indentations; scatter the onion over the top of the dough. Drizzle the remaining 2 tablespoons oil over the dough; cover and let rise 30 minutes. Bake at 400°F for 24 to 26 minutes or until the bread is golden and cooked through. Cool in the pan for 6 to 8 minutes. Turn the bread out; slice and serve.

BONUS
ENTERTAINING
MENUS

It's not easy to find room in a tight budget for holiday meals and other special occasions. But it's not impossible! Armed with my tightwad shopping tips and a little DIY ingenuity, you can set out a gorgeous holiday feast and throw a smashing party without breaking the bank. You'll even have room in the budget to create a couple of beautiful, festive, and super-tasty signature cocktails—one for each occasion. Same goes for a pair of desserts that'll wow.

Total cost
$24.92

Serves 6 to 8

$25 Small Plates Party

When I entertain, I like to try new and interesting recipes and cooking techniques. It's a delicate balance of creating food that's deliciously different but not so much so as to be off-putting. Obviously, I want to impress, but more important, I want guests to feel comfortable and welcome in my home. And I definitely want everyone to have a great time.

The first rule of entertaining on a budget? Don't sacrifice flavor. Go big and bold. With flavors, that is. That way portions can be small, but they won't seem meager. Host a Small Plates Party, for example. As in the Mediterranean tradition (called *tapas* in Spain and *meze* in Greece), offer small tastes of a variety of dishes instead of hosting a traditional sit-down dinner party.

Start with a signature cocktail and set out two or three snacks for the first 45 minutes of your party. Then bring out your heavier hors d'oeuvres. Finally, enlist your guests' help in cooking dessert. Here's how you can do all that for under $25.

MENU

Cucumber-Mint
Tequila Tonic

Pecan-Maple-Bacon
Popcorn

Rosemary-Walnut
Cheese Wafers

Olive & Walnut
Tapenade Crostini

Sesame-Soy Meatballs

Beet & Brown
Rice Sliders

Maple-Glazed
Donut Holes

Total Cost $5.96

Cucumber-Mint Tequila Tonic

HANDS-ON **15 MIN.** TOTAL **15 MIN.**
MAKES **ABOUT 2 CUPS**

Cucumber-Mint Tequila Tonic is the perfect cocktail: It's cool and refreshing during the warmer months. And in the winter, it'll make you feel as if you're sitting beachside without a care in the world. Alcohol is expensive, so serving a signature cocktail is a luxury. Silver or blanco tequila is less expensive than the darker aged varieties.

2 cups chopped English cucumber
$1/2$ cup fresh mint leaves
$1/3$ cup agave nectar
$1/4$ cup fresh cilantro leaves
1 lime, sectioned and juiced
Dash of salt
$1/2$ cup tequila blanco
$3/4$ cup chilled tonic water

Place the first 6 ingredients in a food processor; pulse until smooth. Scrape the mixture into a liquid measuring cup; stir in the tequila. Strain the mixture through a fine sieve into a serving pitcher, pressing to release all the liquid. Chill or serve over ice. Stir in the tonic water just before serving.

🏷️ TIGHTWAD TIP
Buying Tequila

Look for Lunazul brand tequila. It's less expensive than some of the premium brands, but it works great in this cocktail because of its tropical, peppery, grassy flavor notes.

Total Cost: $2.49

Pecan-Maple-Bacon Popcorn

HANDS-ON 15 MIN.
TOTAL 1 HR., 15 MIN.
MAKES ABOUT 8 CUPS

1 tablespoon canola oil

2 tablespoons bacon drippings, divided

4 ounces popping corn

1 tablespoon unsalted butter

1/2 cup packed light brown sugar

2 tablespoons pure maple syrup

1/4 teaspoon baking soda

1/2 cup chopped lightly toasted pecans

1 large egg white, lightly beaten

1 teaspoon kosher salt

Cooking spray

1. Preheat the oven to 225°F.

2. Heat a medium saucepan with a tight-fitting lid over medium-high heat. Add the oil and 1 tablespoon bacon drippings to the pan; swirl to coat. Add the popping corn to the pan; cover with the lid, and shake the pan to coat the corn in hot oil. Cook the popcorn for 3 to 5 minutes or until the popping begins to slow, shaking the pan occasionally. Remove from the heat.

3. Melt the butter in a small saucepan over medium-high heat; stir in the brown sugar and maple syrup. Cook, stirring often, until the sugar dissolves, about 1 minute. Boil 1 minute without stirring. Remove from the heat; stir in the remaining 1 tablespoon bacon drippings, baking soda, and pecans. Drizzle the pecan mixture over the popped corn; toss. Add the egg white to the popcorn mixture; sprinkle with salt. Toss well to coat.

4. Spread the popcorn mixture in a single layer on a foil-lined baking sheet coated with cooking spray. Bake at 225°F for 30 minutes; stir. Bake for 20 more minutes or until the popcorn is dry and crisp. Cool to room temperature, and store in an airtight container for 2 to 3 weeks.

Total Cost: $3.28

Rosemary-Walnut Cheese Wafers

HANDS-ON 15 MIN.
TOTAL 1 HR., 45 MIN.
MAKES 32 WAFERS

1 cup all-purpose flour (about 4.5 ounces)

1/2 teaspoon kosher salt

1/4 teaspoon baking powder

1/4 teaspoon garlic powder

1/4 teaspoon chopped fresh rosemary leaves

1/8 teaspoon ground cayenne pepper

1/2 cup cold unsalted butter, cut into small pieces

3/4 cup shredded sharp cheddar cheese

1/3 cup chopped lightly toasted walnuts

1/4 cup grated Parmesan cheese

1. Weigh or lightly spoon the flour into a dry measuring cup; level with a knife. Combine the flour and the next 5 ingredients in a bowl, stirring well to combine. Place the butter and remaining ingredients in the bowl of a heavy-duty stand mixer; beat at medium speed with the paddle attachment until creamy. With the motor running at low speed, slowly add the flour mixture, beating until well blended, scraping the sides as needed.

2. Divide the dough into two equal portions. Roll each portion into a cylinder with a diameter of 1 1/2 inches; wrap in plastic. Chill at least 1 hour or up to a week.

3. Preheat the oven to 375°F. Line a baking sheet with parchment paper.

4. Slice the dough into 1/4-inch-thick rounds, and place 2 inches apart on the prepared baking sheet. Bake at 375°F for 15 to 18 minutes or until the wafers are golden and crisp. Cool for 5 minutes on the baking sheet. Remove the wafers to a wire rack; cool completely. Store in an airtight container for up to a week.

Note: Be sure you allow time to chill the dough before you slice and bake, so the wafers will hold their shape in the hot oven.

Sesame-Soy
Meatballs

Cucumber-Mint
Tequila Tonic

Olive & Walnut
Tapenade Crostini

Pecan-Maple-
Bacon Popcorn

Rosemary-Walnut Cheese Wafers

Beet & Brown
Rice Sliders

Olive & Walnut Tapenade Crostini

HANDS-ON **10 MIN.** TOTAL **15 MIN.**
MAKES **12 CROSTINI**

When briny, salty olives are blitzed with toasted walnuts, tangy Dijon mustard, and pungent garlic and shallots, irresistible tapenade (or olive spread) is the result. Smear a bit on bread slices for a lovely appetizer, or serve it with grilled chicken or pork for a quick and easy, budget-friendly dinner.

2 tablespoons chopped fresh flat-leaf parsley leaves, divided

1/2 cup pitted kalamata olives

1/3 cup chopped toasted walnuts

1 tablespoon chopped shallot

1 1/4 teaspoons minced fresh garlic

1 teaspoon Dijon mustard

1/2 teaspoon grated fresh lemon zest

3 tablespoon extra-virgin olive oil, divided

1/4 teaspoon kosher salt

1/4 teaspoon black pepper

1 (4-ounce) piece French baguette bread, cut into 12 slices

1. Arrange the top rack of the oven 7 inches from the broiler element. Preheat the broiler to high.

2. Place 1 1/2 tablespoons parsley, olives, and the next 5 ingredients in a mini chopper or food processor; pulse 4 to 6 times or until the mixture is coarsely ground, scraping the sides as needed. Drizzle 1 tablespoon oil through the food chute; pulse until blended. Repeat the process with 1 tablespoon oil; pulse until combined. Season with salt and pepper.

3. Brush the remaining 1 tablespoon oil over the baguette slices; arrange in a single layer on a broiler-safe baking sheet. Broil for 2 to 3 minutes or just until lightly toasted. Spread about 2 teaspoons tapenade over each toasted baguette slice; sprinkle with the remaining 1 1/2 teaspoons chopped parsley.

Sesame-Soy Meatballs

HANDS-ON **30 MIN.** TOTAL **37 MIN.**
MAKES **20 MEATBALLS**

Traditional meatballs are infused with salty, sweet, and a little heat for a fantastic party offering. Kick up the sweet and heat by serving with pepper jelly as a dipping sauce. I love Trader Joe's pepper jelly—the jars are plentiful and affordable.

1 green onion, minced

1 tablespoon brown sugar

1 1/2 tablespoons lower-sodium soy sauce

1 tablespoon dark sesame oil

1 1/2 teaspoons sambal oelek (ground fresh chile paste)

1/8 teaspoon salt

3 garlic cloves, finely minced

1/2 pound 80% lean ground beef

Cooking spray

1/2 cup hot and sweet pepper jelly (such as Trader Joe's)

1. Preheat the oven to 400°F.

2. Combine the first 7 ingredients in a large mixing bowl. Add the beef; mix gently to combine. With moist hands, shape the beef mixture into 20 meatballs.

3. Heat a large cast-iron skillet over medium-high heat. Add half of the meatballs to the pan; cook 4 minutes, turning to brown the meatballs on all sides. Arrange the browned meatballs in a single layer on a jelly-roll pan coated with cooking spray. Repeat the procedure with the remaining meatballs. Bake the meatballs at 400°F for 7 minutes or until done. Serve with the pepper jelly for dipping.

Total Cost: $4.65

Beet & Brown Rice Sliders

HANDS-ON **55 MIN.**
TOTAL **1 HR., 15 MIN.**
MAKES **8 SLIDERS**

Red beets give these meatless slider patties the look of a real beef burger. Toasted walnuts and chewy brown rice add texture and delicious flavor.

16 thin slices sourdough bread

Cooking spray

1 cup cooked cooled whole-grain brown rice blend

6 tablespoons grated cooked red beet

¼ cup panko breadcrumbs

3 tablespoons chopped toasted walnuts

2 tablespoons chopped fresh flat-leaf parsley

1 tablespoon finely chopped shallot

½ teaspoon kosher salt

¼ teaspoon freshly ground black pepper

1 tablespoon Dijon mustard

1 large egg

2 tablespoons olive oil, divided

1 ½ ounces goat cheese

1 cup baby arugula

1. Arrange the top rack of the oven 7 inches from the broiler element. Preheat the broiler to high.

2. Cut each bread slice into a 3-inch circle using a round cutter; reserve the scraps for another use (such as breadcrumbs or croutons). Lightly coat the bread rounds with cooking spray. Arrange the bread rounds in a single layer on a baking sheet. Broil 2 minutes on each side or until lightly toasted. Cool on a wire rack.

3. Reduce the oven temperature to 400°F. Place a baking sheet in the oven to preheat.

4. Combine the rice and the next 7 ingredients in a medium bowl. Combine the mustard and egg, stirring well. Add the egg mixture to the rice mixture; stir until well blended. Divide the rice mixture into 8 equal portions. Working with one portion at a time, spoon each portion into a 2 ½-inch round cookie cutter; pack the mixture down. Remove the mold. Repeat the procedure 7 times to form 8 patties.

5. Heat a large skillet over medium-high heat. Add 1 tablespoon oil to the pan; swirl to coat. Carefully add 4 patties to the pan; cook 2 minutes. Carefully transfer the patties to the preheated baking sheet, turning the patties over and arranging in a single layer. Repeat the procedure with the remaining 1 tablespoon oil and remaining 4 patties. Place the pan in the oven; bake at 400°F for 9 minutes. Divide the cheese evenly among the patties; bake 1 more minute or until the cheese is soft and the patties are set.

6. Place 8 toasted bread rounds on a flat surface; top each round with 1 patty. Divide the arugula evenly among the sliders; top with the remaining toasted bread rounds.

TIGHTWAD TIPS
For the Hostess

1. Timing is everything: Think of the first half hour to 45 minutes as cocktail hour, and serve snacks and drinks while you wait for all your guests to arrive.

2. Station someone at the bar to be in charge of pouring (and rationing) the signature cocktail. Be sure to have appropriately sized glasses and plenty of ice.

3. Make the bar inviting, and give the appearance of abundance with personal touches. Keep a couple of pitchers of ice water available at all times. Start with tap water, but float a few mint leaves, cucumber slices, and unexpected fresh fruits in the pitcher. Skip citrus and berries and try thin slices of fresh peach or pear or pomegranate arils instead. Slice limes to garnish the cocktails. Set extra tonic water on the bar, and offer any sodas you have on hand.

4. During the cocktail hour, be sure everyone has a beverage first thing. Next, draw people away from the bar, and (if you're like me) you'll want them out of the kitchen too. So, set the snacks around your home in places where people can comfortably sit or stand and chat. Make small cones out of pretty paper (or use regular parchment paper) to portion the popcorn and make it last.

5. Once everyone arrives (or an hour in), set the sliders and meatballs out buffet-style. Use small plates for guests—appetizer size works well. Keep the (less costly) snacks, like popcorn and cheese wafers out and available to guests throughout the party and move them to the buffet with the main dishes. Set the popcorn cones in juice glasses or silver julep cups on the buffet.

6. Add drama, height, and color to the buffet to keep things festive. Don't feel like you need to buy anything new. Instead, mix and match serveware, silverware, plates, and glasses, and make do with what you have. Cut fresh, colorful flowers from your yard and put them in bud vases sprinkled throughout the buffet.

TIGHTWAD TIPS
Party Extras

• Make your donut dough ahead and have it ready to go after everyone's eaten. Now's the time to take the party into the kitchen. Assign everyone a job: someone to portion and someone to roll the dough balls, one or two people on the fryer, and another couple of people to make the glaze and dunk the donut holes when they're done.

• Let guests know ahead of time that you'll provide a signature cocktail to get the party started, but encourage them to bring something to help stock the bar. I love the idea of an organized tasting: Ask guests to bring beer, wine, or a spirit of your choosing. Be as vague or specific as you wish. For example, ask guests to bring their favorite sparkling wine, or ask them to bring their favorite sauvignon blanc. And be prepared to share with the group.

Total Cost: $2.49

Maple-Glazed Donut Holes

HANDS-ON **35 MIN.**
TOTAL **2 HR., 5 MIN.**
MAKES **20 DONUT HOLES**

The key to perfect donut holes is temperature, so use a candy thermometer. Be patient and let the oil get up to temp before you start frying, and allow it to return to the proper temperature between each batch.

3 tablespoons warm water (100° to 110°F)

2 tablespoons granulated sugar

¾ teaspoon active dry yeast

⅔ cup all-purpose flour (about 3 ounces)

⅛ teaspoon salt

1½ tablespoons sour cream

1 large egg, lightly beaten

Cooking spray

3 cups peanut oil

¾ cup powdered sugar

1 tablespoon pure maple syrup

1. Combine the first 3 ingredients in a large bowl. Let stand 5 minutes or until bubbly. Weigh or lightly spoon the flour into a dry measuring cup, and level with a knife. Combine the flour and salt. Add the sour cream and egg to the yeast mixture; stir until smooth. Add the flour mixture; stir until a moist dough forms.

2. Turn the dough out onto a lightly floured surface. Knead until smooth and elastic, about 3 minutes (the dough will feel slightly sticky). Place the dough in a clean bowl coated with cooking spray. Cover the dough with plastic wrap. Let rise in a warm place (85°F), free from drafts, 1 hour or until almost doubled in size.

3. Punch the dough down. Divide the dough into 20 equal portions; roll each portion into a ball. Cover the dough with plastic wrap coated with cooking spray; let stand for 30 minutes.

4. Clip a candy/fry thermometer onto the side of a Dutch oven; add the oil to the pan. Heat the oil to 375°F. Combine the powdered sugar, maple syrup, and 1 tablespoon water, whisking until smooth. Place 6 to 7 dough balls in the hot oil; fry 2 minutes or until golden and done, turning as necessary. Make sure the oil temperature remains at 375°F. Remove the donut holes from the pan using a slotted spoon; drain. Dip the donut holes into the syrup mixture; remove with a slotted spoon. Drain on a cooling rack over a baking sheet. Repeat the procedure 2 times with the remaining dough balls and syrup mixture.

Serves 8

$50 Thanksgiving

Total cost $49.68

As much as I love Thanksgiving—and I do love an opportunity to stop and say grace for my many blessings—it's a tricky holiday for the cook.

That last bit may have you scratching your head, right? Because everyone knows you serve turkey and potatoes. If you grew up in the South (or Texas), like I did, there'll be some sweet potatoes on the table too. A green veggie and salad of some sort. And pie or cake. Maybe both. Done.

Do you see the problem? When you basically serve the same meal, year after year, how do you vary it enough to keep things interesting and fresh—without killing yourself, that is? And it goes without saying: You have to keep the costs in check too.

Not to worry one little bit. Here's a menu that you (the cook) and your family will all agree is a winner. I've even added a few notes to help you plan your prep, so you can get it all done with minimal stress. You may just love it so much, you'll want to hold onto the recipes and do it again next year. Exactly the same way.

MENU

Citrus-Pomegranate Sparkler

Sweet Potato & Pumpkin Bisque with Peppery Pepita Brittle

Speedy Apple-Beet Salad

Potatoes au Gratin

Roasted Brussels Sprouts with Bacon & Pecans

Butter-Basted Turkey

Red Velvet Cake

Total Cost $7.83

Citrus-Pomegranate Sparkler

HANDS-ON **10 MIN.**
TOTAL **4 HR., 25 MIN.**
MAKES **ABOUT 4 CUPS**

¼ cup sugar

¾ cup vodka

1 cup unsweetened pomegranate juice

½ cup fresh orange juice (about 2 medium oranges)

¼ cup fresh lime juice (about 2 medium limes)

¼ cup fresh lemon juice (about 2 medium lemons)

1½ cups chilled sparkling wine (such as Spanish cava)

Fresh orange slices (optional)

1. Stir the sugar into ¼ cup water in a (4-cup) microwave-safe liquid measuring cup. Microwave at HIGH power for 4 minutes or until sugar dissolves, stirring every minute. Cool slightly, about 15 minutes. Stir the vodka and juices into the syrup; cover and chill until cold, at least 4 hours.

2. Divide the juice mixture among 8 ice-filled cocktail glasses; top each serving with sparkling wine. Garnish with fresh orange slices, if desired.

Note: Buy the least-expensive vodka for this cocktail.

TIGHTWAD TIP
Budget-Friendly Bubbly

Cava is Spain's version of Champagne, and it's generally the best-tasting affordable sparkling wine.

Total Cost $3.36

Sweet Potato & Pumpkin Bisque

HANDS-ON **30 MIN.** TOTAL **1 HR.**
MAKES **MAKES ABOUT 5 CUPS**

This soup is super simple to prepare, but the flavor is anything but simple. Make the brittle one to two days ahead and keep it in a parchment-lined airtight container at room temperature until you're ready to serve.

2 tablespoons unsalted butter

$^2/_3$ cup chopped yellow onion (about 1 small onion)

$^1/_3$ cup chopped carrot (about 1 medium carrot)

1 tablespoon chopped fresh garlic (about 3 cloves)

2 teaspoons tomato paste

1 (8-ounce) sweet potato, peeled and chopped

2 tablespoons honey

$^3/_4$ teaspoon kosher salt

$^1/_2$ teaspoon ground cumin

$^1/_4$ teaspoon ground cinnamon

$^1/_8$ teaspoon black pepper

Pinch of ground cayenne pepper

3 cups Overnight Chicken Stock (page 218) or store-bought

$^1/_2$ cup heavy cream

1 cup canned pumpkin

$^1/_2$ cup half-and-half

$^1/_4$ cup crushed Peppery Pepita Brittle (at right) or toasted pumpkinseed kernels

1. Melt the butter in a medium saucepan over medium-high heat. Add the onion and carrot; cook until softened and lightly browned, about 3 minutes, stirring frequently. Add the garlic and tomato paste; cook 30 seconds, stirring constantly. Stir in the sweet potato, honey, salt, cumin, cinnamon, black pepper, and cayenne; cook for 1 to 2 minutes, stirring occasionally. Stir in the stock, cream, and pumpkin; bring to a boil. Reduce the heat to medium, and simmer for 20 to 25 minutes or until all the ingredients are very tender, stirring occasionally. Let stand for 10 to 15 minutes or until cooled slightly.

2. Pour the mixture into a blender; process until smooth. Stir in the half-and-half. Season to taste with salt and pepper. Divide the soup among serving bowls; garnish each serving with the brittle.

Peppery Pepita Brittle

Melt 1 tablespoon unsalted butter in a small saucepan over medium heat. Add $^1/_2$ cup unsalted pumpkinseed kernels (pepitas), $^1/_4$ teaspoon kosher salt, $^1/_8$ teaspoon freshly ground black pepper, a pinch of ground cumin, and a pinch of ground cayenne pepper to the pan, and cook 3 minutes, stirring frequently. Set aside. Combine $^1/_3$ cup sugar, 2 $^1/_2$ tablespoons light-colored corn syrup, and 2 $^1/_2$ tablespoons water in a very small, heavy saucepan over medium-high heat; bring to a boil, stirring just until the sugar dissolves. Cook until a candy thermometer registers 325°F, about 5 to 6 minutes.

Remove the pan from the heat; add the pumpkinseed mixture and $^3/_8$ teaspoon baking soda. Working quickly, spread the mixture in a thin, even layer on a baking sheet lined with parchment paper; let stand until set, about 20 minutes. Break into pieces.

Countdown to T-Day

5 DAYS BEFORE

- Shop

3 DAYS BEFORE

- Prepare Sweet Potato & Pumpkin Bisque. Cool, cover, and chill.
- Prepare Potatoes au Gratin.

2 DAYS BEFORE

- Prepare Citrus-Pomegranate Sparkler through step 1. Cover and chill. Chill sparkling wine.
- Bake cake layers; cool completely, and wrap with plastic.

1 DAY BEFORE

- Make Peppery Pepita Brittle. Cool and store in airtight container.
- Prep ingredients for Roasted Brussels Sprouts with Bacon & Pecans.
- Frost the cake.

THANKSGIVING

- Prepare Butter-Basted Turkey.
- Cook the Brussels sprouts.
- Reheat the potatoes and soup.
- Prepare Speedy Apple-Beet Salad.
- Add sparkling wine to the cocktail just before serving.

Citrus-
Pomegranate
Sparkler

Speedy Apple-
Beet Salad

Butter-
Basted Turkey

Sweet Potato &
Pumpkin Bisque

Roasted Brussels
Sprouts with
Bacon & Pecans

Potatoes
au Gratin

Speedy Apple-Beet Salad

HANDS-ON **13 MIN.**
TOTAL **13 MIN.** SERVES **8**

Hooray for the food processor, which makes this crisp, refreshing salad a snap to make. Don't make this dish too far ahead, as it might discolor; aim for no more than 30 minutes before you plan to serve it. My local supermarket usually carries golden beets—which have a milder flavor than the super-earthy red ones—but I always find them at Whole Foods.

2 red-skinned apples, unpeeled, cored, and cut into thin wedges

1/4 cup fresh lemon juice

1 tablespoon sugar

2 medium-sized golden beets, peeled and cut into wedges

1/4 small red onion, cut into 2 wedges

1/3 cup fresh flat-leaf parsley leaves

1/2 teaspoon kosher salt

1/4 teaspoon black pepper

2 tablespoons canola oil

1 1/2 tablespoons Dijon mustard

1/2 cup toasted walnut halves

1/4 cup crumbled blue cheese

Combine the apples, lemon juice, and sugar in a large bowl; toss to coat. Slice the beet and onion wedges in the food processor fitted with a slicing blade; add the beet mixture and parsley to the apple mixture. Sprinkle with salt and pepper. Stir in the oil and mustard; toss gently to coat. Arrange about 2/3 cup salad on each of 8 plates; top each with 1 tablespoon walnuts and about 1 1/2 teaspoons cheese.

Potatoes au Gratin

HANDS-ON **30 MIN.**
TOTAL **2 HR.** SERVES **8**

Yukon Gold potatoes are perfect for this classic crowd-pleasing side dish because of their naturally buttery flavor and moderate level of starch. You can make the potatoes up to three days before Thanksgiving, cool, cover, and keep them refrigerated until the big day. To reheat, pull the dish out and let it stand at room temperature while the oven preheats, cover the dish with foil, and bake until hot. Uncover and bake another 5 to 10 minutes if you need to brown the top before serving.

Cooking spray

2 cups heavy cream

1/2 cup Overnight Chicken Stock (page 218) or store-bought

5 garlic cloves, smashed

1 shallot, coarsely chopped

1 (1-ounce) package poultry herbs

1 (2-ounce) chunk Parmigiano-Reggiano cheese with rind

3 pounds Yukon Gold potatoes, peeled and thinly sliced

1 1/2 teaspoons kosher salt

3/4 teaspoon black pepper

1/2 cup shredded Gruyère cheese

1. Preheat the oven to 350°F. Coat an 11- x 7-inch baking dish with cooking spray; set aside.

2. Combine the cream, stock, garlic, and shallot in a small saucepan. Add 1 sprig fresh rosemary and 1 sprig fresh sage to pan with cream. Chop 2 teaspoons fresh thyme leaves; set aside. Reserve the remaining poultry herbs for another use. Cut the rind from the cheese, taking off as little lighter-colored cheese as possible. Add the rind to the cream mixture; bring to a boil over medium-high heat. Remove from the heat; let stand 5 minutes. Grate the Parmigiano-Reggiano cheese; set aside.

3. Strain the cream through a fine-mesh sieve; discard the solids. Spoon 1/2 cup cream into the prepared dish. Arrange one-third of the potato slices in a single layer over the cream in the prepared dish, arranging them in an overlapping, shingle fashion; sprinkle the potatoes with 1/2 teaspoon salt, 1/4 teaspoon pepper, and 1/4 cup Parmigiano-Reggiano. Repeat the layers. Arrange the remaining potatoes slices on top; sprinkle with remaining 1/2 teaspoon salt and 1/4 teaspoon pepper. Pour the remaining cream over the potatoes.

4. Cover the dish with foil, and bake at 350°F for 1 hour. Uncover; top with the Gruyère cheese and 1 teaspoon thyme. Bake 30 more minutes or until golden brown, bubbly, and the tip of a paring knife slides easily through potatoes. Sprinkle the remaining 1 teaspoon chopped fresh thyme over the top.

Total Cost $4.49

Roasted Brussels Sprouts with Bacon & Pecans

HANDS-ON **15 MIN.**
TOTAL **30 MIN.** SERVES **8**

This fantastic side dish will make Brussels sprouts fans out of the haters.

2 slices bacon

2 tablespoons butter, softened

2 pounds Brussels sprouts, trimmed and halved

1 teaspoon kosher salt

1/4 teaspoon black pepper

1 tablespoon honey

1/2 cup coarsely chopped toasted pecans

1 teaspoon grated fresh lemon zest

2 tablespoons chopped fresh flat-leaf parsley

1. Preheat the oven to 400°F.

2. Place the bacon on a rimmed baking sheet, and bake at 400°F until crisp, 10 to 12 minutes. Transfer the bacon to paper towels to drain, reserving the drippings in the pan. Add the butter to the pan; swirl to melt. Add the Brussels sprouts to the pan; toss to coat. Add the salt, pepper, and honey; toss. Bake at 400°F until tender and slightly charred, 15 to 18 minutes. Toss with the pecans and zest; spoon the Brussels sprouts into a serving bowl.

3. Crumble the bacon. Top the Brussels sprouts with the crumbled bacon and parsley.

Total Cost $9.88

Butter-Basted Turkey

HANDS-ON **25 MIN.**
TOTAL **2 HR., 55 MIN.**
SERVES **8 TO 10**

Rub a tasty butter mixture under the skin directly over the flesh, so all the flavors seep into the meat as it cooks. Then baste with melted butter as it cooks for a gorgeously crisp skin and mind-blowingly juicy and delicious turkey.

3/4 cup butter, divided

3 tablespoons minced shallots

1 tablespoon chopped fresh thyme leaves

2 teaspoons chopped fresh sage

1 teaspoon grated fresh lemon zest

4 garlic cloves, minced into paste

1 tablespoon plus 1 teaspoon kosher salt, divided

1/2 teaspoon black pepper

1 (10-pound) whole turkey

1 tablespoon cornstarch

1/4 cup Overnight Chicken Stock (page 218) or store-bought

1. Melt 1/2 cup butter in a saucepan over medium heat. Remove the pan from the heat; skim the milk solids from the top of the melted butter. Slowly pour the butter out of the pan, leaving the remaining solids in the bottom of the pan. Combine the remaining 1/4 cup butter, shallots, and the next 4 ingredients; add 1 teaspoon kosher salt and the pepper. Beat the butter mixture with an electric mixer at medium speed until well combined.

2. Preheat the oven to 325°F.

3. Remove the giblets and neck from the turkey; reserve for another use. Pat turkey dry. Separate the turkey skin from the flesh over the breast and legs. Rub the butter-shallot mixture under the skin over the flesh. Lift the wing tips up and over the back; tuck under turkey. Tie the legs together with kitchen string. Brush the turkey with the clarified butter; sprinkle with the remaining 1 tablespoon kosher salt. Place a roasting rack in a large roasting pan. Arrange turkey, breast side up, on the roasting rack. Bake at 325°F for 1 hour and 30 minutes, basting every 20 minutes.

4. Increase the oven temperature to 450°F (do not remove the turkey from the oven); bake 25 more minutes or until a thermometer inserted into meaty part of a thigh registers 165°F. Remove turkey from the oven, reserving the drippings in the pan; let the turkey stand for 30 minutes before carving.

5. Place the roasting pan over medium-high heat. Whisk the cornstarch into the stock; add to the drippings in the pan. Bring to a boil. Cook 1 minute or until slightly thickened, whisking often. Remove from the heat, and season to taste with salt and pepper.

TIGHTWAD TIP
Buying a Whole Turkey

For the best value, look for frozen whole turkeys at Walmart. They carry young antibiotic-free turkeys that are raised by family farms.

Dinner Extra:

To decorate your table, keep it simple. Clip camellias and float them in water for a minimalist fresh floral arrangement; scatter magnolia leaves on the table to fill in or even paint some silver or gold; or create a still life centerpiece in a silver or other fancy bowl using a mix of seasonal citrus and a few pine cones from your yard.

Total Cost $10.07

Red Velvet Cake

HANDS-ON **30 MIN.** TOTAL **3 HR.**
SERVES **8 TO 10**

I've loved red velvet cake for as long as I can remember. In fact, it's the cake my grandmother used to make every year for my birthday. It's now my son's favorite cake. Needless to say, I've had a few different versions of this classic. Hands down, this recipe yields the best, moist, delicate cake I've tasted. And it makes a truly glorious finale for your Turkey Day dinner.

CAKE

Baking spray with flour

2 cups granulated sugar

3/4 cup unsalted butter, softened

1/2 cup canola oil

3 large eggs

1 1/3 cups all-purpose flour (about 6 ounces)

1 1/4 cups cake flour (about 5 ounces)

2 tablespoons unsweetened cocoa

1 1/2 teaspoons baking soda

3/4 teaspoon salt

1 cup buttermilk

1/2 cup sour cream

2 teaspoons pure vanilla extract

2 tablespoons red liquid food coloring

1 tablespoon cider vinegar

FROSTING

3/4 cup unsalted butter, softened

2 (8-ounce) blocks cream cheese, softened

1/2 teaspoon pure vanilla extract

1/4 teaspoon salt

6 to 8 cups powdered sugar

1. To prepare the cake, preheat the oven to 350°F. Coat 3 (8-inch) round cake pans with baking spray with flour; set aside.

2. Place the granulated sugar, 3/4 cup butter, and oil in the bowl of a heavy-duty stand mixer; beat at medium-high speed until very light and fluffy, about 3 minutes, scraping the sides of the bowl as needed. Add the eggs, one at a time, beating until incorporated after each addition.

3. Weigh or lightly spoon flours into dry measuring cups; level with a knife. Combine the flours, cocoa, baking soda, and 3/4 teaspoon salt in a bowl, stirring well. Whisk together the buttermilk and the next 3 ingredients. Add the dry ingredients alternately with the buttermilk mixture, beginning and ending with the dry ingredients, beating at low speed just until blended and scraping the sides and bottom of the bowl as needed. Fold in the vinegar.

4. Divide the batter evenly among the prepared pans; bake at 350°F for 22 to 28 minutes or until a wooden pick inserted into the center of the cake comes out clean. Cool for 5 minutes in the pans. Turn the cakes out onto wire racks; cool completely, about 1 hour.

5. To prepare the frosting, beat 3/4 cup butter and the cream cheese at medium-high speed with an electric mixer until light and fluffy. Beat in the vanilla and salt. Add 6 cups powdered sugar, 1 cup at a time, beating until smooth after each addition and scraping the sides of the bowl as needed. Add enough of the remaining 2 cups powdered sugar, 1/2 cup at a time, if needed, until the frosting reaches the desired consistency.

6. To assemble, place one layer on a cake stand; top with about 1/4 cup frosting. Repeat with the remaining 2 layers, ending with a cake layer. Spread a thin layer of frosting over the sides and the top of the cake to form a crumb coat; chill for 30 minutes. Carefully and gently spread the remaining frosting over the sides and on the top of the cake. Refrigerate until ready to serve. Let the cake stand at room temperature for 30 minutes before slicing and serving.

TIGHTWAD TIP
Neutral-flavored Oil

Adding a bit of oil to a cake works wonders for the texture. Canola oil is so cheap, and it has a neutral flavor, which lets the buttery flavor in this cake shine through.

Metric Equivalents

COOKING/OVEN TEMPERATURES

	Fahrenheit	Celsius	Gas Mark
Freeze Water	32° F	0° C	
Room Temp.	68° F	20° C	
Boil Water	212° F	100° C	
Bake	325° F	160° C	3
	350° F	180° C	4
	375° F	190° C	5
	400° F	200° C	6
	425° F	220° C	7
	450° F	230° C	8
Broil			Grill

LIQUID INGREDIENTS BY VOLUME

¼ tsp					=	1 ml		
½ tsp					=	2 ml		
1 tsp					=	5 ml		
3 tsp	=	1 Tbsp	=	½ fl oz	=	15 ml		
2 Tbsp	=	⅛ cup	=	1 fl oz	=	30 ml		
4 Tbsp	=	¼ cup	=	2 fl oz	=	60 ml		
5⅓ Tbsp	=	⅓ cup	=	3 fl oz	=	80 ml		
8 Tbsp	=	½ cup	=	4 fl oz	=	120 ml		
10⅔ Tbsp	=	⅔ cup	=	5 fl oz	=	160 ml		
12 Tbsp	=	¾ cup	=	6 fl oz	=	180 ml		
16 Tbsp	=	1 cup	=	8 fl oz	=	240 ml		
1 pt	=	2 cups	=	16 fl oz	=	480 ml		
1 qt	=	4 cups	=	32 fl oz	=	960 ml		
				33 fl oz	=	1000 ml	=	1 l

DRY INGREDIENTS BY WEIGHT

(To convert ounces to grams, multiply the number of ounces by 30.)

1 oz	=	¹⁄₁₆ lb	=	30 g
4 oz	=	¼ lb	=	120 g
8 oz	=	½ lb	=	240 g
12 oz	=	¾ lb	=	360 g
16 oz	=	1 lb	=	480 g

LENGTH

(To convert inches to centimeters, multiply inches by 2.5.)

1 in				=	2.5 cm	
12 in	=	1 ft		=	30 cm	
36 in	=	3 ft	=	1 yd	=	90 cm
40 in	=				100 cm	= 1 m

EQUIVALENTS FOR DIFFERENT TYPES OF INGREDIENTS

Standard Cup	Fine Powder (ex. flour)	Grain (ex. rice)	Granular (ex. sugar)	Liquid Solids (ex. butter)	Liquid (ex. milk)
1	140 g	150 g	190 g	200 g	240 ml
¾	105 g	113 g	143 g	150 g	180 ml
⅔	93 g	100 g	125 g	133 g	160 ml
½	70 g	75 g	95 g	100 g	120 ml
⅓	47 g	50 g	63 g	67 g	80 ml
¼	35 g	38 g	48 g	50 g	60 ml
⅛	18 g	19 g	24 g	25 g	30 ml

Index

Acknowledgments

The book you're holding is a labor of love. And dedication and countless shopping trips to every store and market imaginable. An exhaustive search, if you will, all in the service of finding the absolute lowest prices on the best ingredients, so you can feed your family and friends the most delicious meals possible. All the while keeping your grocery budget in check.

Although my name appears on the cover, this project is most certainly a decades-long team effort. With input and influence from family, friends, and co-workers past and present. I'll start at the start—with family—in expressing my gratitude.

Mom, thanks for all that you've sacrificed so your daughters can have the opportunities and lives we live today. Thank you, too, for passing on, "The Good Stuff Rule," without which this book wouldn't exist. It goes something like this: Eschew the cheap, lazy, easy and predictable. Opt instead for well-made, hand-crafted, home-grown finer things in life. As it applies to food—and these pages in particular—this principle is the heart and soul of this book. Budgeting is tedious and boring, and it isn't all that difficult if you're willing to slash whole categories of foods from your list of options. Which, of course, is absolutely no fun. I prefer to have a little fun, so these pages show how you can include "The Good Stuff" in your meals without busting your budget.

I also owe a debt of gratitude to both of my grandmothers. They're the ones who taught me to cook. And so much more. To my son: Thank you, Matthew, for being the pickiest eater I've ever cooked for. You've taught me how to be more imaginative with a few select ingredients. And thank you, too, for being a discerning taste tester of mom's recipes. And for your growing interest in good food and your help in the kitchen. You're my favorite sous chef! To my husband Tim: Thank you for your love and support. And for last-minute runs to the store and dishes. Oh the many dishes! And for your patience with me—your crazy creative wife.

To my Southern Progress family: Working at *Southern Living* and *Cooking Light* is one of the greatest honors of my life. And all the wonderful folks I worked alongside changed, influenced, and shaped my life in ways I couldn't have imagined before I was lucky enough to land there for a couple of decades. There are too many of you to name, but you know who you are. From the bottom of my heart, thank you!

To the Oxmoor House team: Rachel West, thank you for bringing this opportunity my way. The process has been difficult and stressful, but worth the effort, I hope. A HUGE thanks to Rachel and the edit team, the photo group, and the Time Inc. Food Studios team for your brilliant and dedicated work. You all made the pages sing.

And to you the reader: Thank you for picking up my little book. Bon appétit!

About the Author

Julie Grimes, a Texas native, grew up learning to cook at her grandmother's apron strings. After culinary school in NYC and a stint at the famed Union Square Café, Julie moved to Birmingham, Alabama, to work at *Southern Living*, where she spent 16 years as a food editor. Her work has also appeared in *Cooking Light*, *Fine Cooking*, *Women's Health*, and many other publications. In 2015, Grimes opened Black Sheep Kitchen, a take-out food business where she and her staff prepare fresh, creative, and delicious classic comfort foods for customers to take, reheat, and enjoy at home.